UNFOLDING CURIOSITY

WRINKLES AND SURPRISES FROM
BUSINESS AND BEYOND

UNFOLDING CURIOSITY

WRINKLES AND SURPRISES FROM BUSINESS AND BEYOND

NANCY K. NAPIER

PUBLISHED BY CCI PRESS
Boise, Idaho

Managing Editor: Madison Motzner
Cover Designer: Zeljka Kojic

ISBN 10: 1546339116
ISBN 13: 978-1546339113

Nancy K. Napier - http://nancyknapier.com/

For anyone who has relentless curiosity in Boise and Beyond

Contents

Preface

Unfolding Curiosity: Wrinkles and Surprises is a selection of blogs and columns published in the *Idaho Statesman* between 2013 and 2017. These small pieces often start with a tiny observation, an experience, or a place where ideas touch, cause friction or joy, and generate unexpected results. They make me think of unfolding a piece of paper, which is often how I write them. I start with an idea, then let it unfold so I can see the wrinkles that create new perspectives, the places where ideas may crease or have fault lines, and the new shapes and surprises that emerge as the paper unfolds.

The book has five sections, each with a loose theme. *Part 1: Learning from Unexpected Sources* draws from fields or ideas that are often far from business to suggest ways that business leaders and others may learn from those unexpected sources. Gymnastics, sumo wrestling, and safari guides become the unexpected places for new views and lessons.

Part 2: Planting Seeds for Creativity and Curiosity includes farming and farmers as places where creativity or curiosity could grow. We do live in an agricultural state, so farming makes good sense to learn from. In addition, the section raises questions from perspectives many of us rarely encounter, such as neuroscience and geophysics, encouraging the notion that we can learn from just about anywhere.

Part 3: Brainstorming New Ideas began with trying to find ways to help different types of businesses find new ideas, whether from other fields or from other countries. We may think of industries like real estate or banking to be fairly stodgy, but that doesn't have to be so, if they—and we—look for ways to make them more creative.

Part 4: Getting Better offers a few tips for busy people, from how to focus and dispel the notion that multitasking is efficient, to finding joy in learning to figuring out what the next steps for a successful career might be.

Part 5: Behind the Scenes offers a few columns about places we've all visited but may not have thought about how they really work--football games and the local zoo. The pieces offer a few surprises and maybe some wrinkles.

If you take away one new thought or tip for action, we'll have achieved the goal. So now go unfold and see the wrinkles!

Part I

Learning from Unexpected Sources

Part 1: Learning from Unexpected Sources taps into concepts that come from fields far beyond business but, might indeed have application for organizational leaders. Sometimes, the furthest afield generate the most interesting. The pieces draw from such areas as gymnastics, sumo wrestling, and African safari guides for unexpected lessons.

No Plaid, No Beard, No Axe—but I Still Can Learn from My Inner Forester

February 8, 2016

I was in Coeur d'Alene in January 2016 at the fifteenth annual Foresters Forum—a very cool get-together for people in the timber industry. They cover topics like wildfire, water quality, silviculture, and legal issues.

Now please know that I don't wear plaid, have a beard, or carry an axe. In my black-leather skirt and scarf, I fit right in. They had no idea I wasn't a forester until I admitted it.

Seriously, I wore that skirt for a reason—to show that I was a world away from them but that in fact we had something in common they didn't realize. I was there to help the more than two hundred foresters start thinking about doing things differently, building teams, and solving problems, just as people in organizations everywhere need to—whether it's the world of timber, sports, or business.

When I was asked to speak to the group, I admitted as I always do, that I knew nothing about the industry or organizations in it but would like to. So I asked a naive question: What do foresters do? And it turns out they can teach the rest of us something about organizational cultures.

Foresters plant seeds or seedlings of trees and nurture them. They try to be sure the environment, including the surrounding soil, helps the trees grow into healthy forests. They watch for trees that become sick and treat them or cull them, to avoid having weak ones destroy the healthy ones. They encourage clusters of trees (forests) to grow, because clumps are likely stronger than a single tree.

Sounds a lot like building a thriving organizational culture to me.

Part of my talk involved having the foresters be creative—a terrible word for people like analytical foresters. Instead, we talked about doing things differently to get better. The example I used was how to stay cool walking about in a climate of "90-90" ninety degrees and ninety percent humidity—think Miami or Houston in August.

In less than five minutes, the people in the room generated more than four hundred ideas. When we got down to what their best were, they had several that seemed like ones that could become real products (e.g., misting drones). Maybe we'll turn those foresters into entrepreneurs.

My point to them was that building a culture in an organization—like building a strong forest—is doable, can be fun, and can make for a higher performing organization, just like a higher performing, or healthier, forest.

Watch out! As a person who enjoys the outdoors from the indoors, I might become dangerous in the wilderness. Yet, who knows? Maybe I have a future career in planting trees.

How Gymnasts Solve Problems on the Fly

January 25, 2016

Do you think you solve problems on the fly? Try it when you are upside down, twelve or fifteen feet in the air, with no net.

If you do something wrong, you could either splat like a bug, face down on the floor, or wrap your back around a four-inch wooden pole. That's what gymnasts face every time when they leap into the air.

When I asked Tina Bird, co-head coach of the Boise State women's gymnastics program, what is different about her sport, she looked at me straight on and said, almost casually, "They solve problems on the fly, literally."

These young women have to know when their hips, feet, or heads might be a few millimeters off, and how to make adjustments to their bodies in the air so they land safely and beautifully. And they do it all in split seconds.

I'm curious about high-performing, highly creative organizations—how they get there and stay that way. The women's gymnastics program at Boise State is one of those. It consistently ranks in the top twenty-five of the sixty-one Division I programs across the United States, and finished at No. 15 in 2016.

With only 180 scholarships available nationwide, and three a year at Boise State, the program can attract the best from inside and outside the United States, including from other countries' national programs (e.g., New Zealand and Peru). The Boise State program's participants have the highest GPA of all of our university's athletic programs. During fall semester 2015, the team broke university record with its 3.82 GPA. In fact, none of the gymnasts had less than a 3.5 GA, and these are students with majors like pre-med, English, and mechanical engineering.

I spent a few hours recently watching the Boise State gymnasts, their three coaches, and their athletic trainer during practices and an intrasquad meet, where the gymnasts compete against each other to determine who will lead the events in team competitions. Whenever I do something like this, I think about what business leaders could learn. Here are a few lessons that will sound familiar to leaders of high-performing organizations:

Have a Magnet

When I asked the students why they joined this program, they immediately tilt their heads toward their coaches. The co-head coaches for the last eight years, Tina Bird and Neil Resnick, informally known as the Bird and Resnick powerhouse team, along with assistant coach Patty Resnick, are hands down the reason young gymnasts are drawn to Boise State.

Before joining Boise State, Patty and Neil Resnick became Master Sports Coaches, an honorary title for coaches who have trained and developed a student who performs at the world competition level or at the Olympics. Neil Resnick still works with the US national team and still trains athletes and their coaches, but his heart and his day job are in Boise. Tina Bird holds records as a gymnast at Boise State, where she competed and became co-head coach in 2007 with Neil Resnick.

Recruit to Your Values

When I asked Bird and Resnick how the program has remained so strong, they immediately said "Culture". We bring in top students who have a passion for the sport and who follow the rules."

That's "all" it is and that's all it is. The program's clear values drive the recruitment.

Of the estimated 68,000 female gymnasts nationwide, only 1,700 reach level ten, the top level, by high school and want to perform in college. That's still a lot of young women chasing 180 scholarships. So the strongest programs can choose the best performers.

Boise coaches also want disciplined, serious students, and since there are no "professional gymnastics" beyond college, they demand that team members put academics first.

Avoid Toxic People

Bird and Resnick also stress staying out of trouble. A few years ago, one of the top-ranked athletes in the conference broke this rule. She became a toxic influence, hurting the team as a whole. So she left the team during the season. The message—stay out of trouble—became even clearer. Since then? High performance, no trouble.

Be Versatile

The best coaches reach individual players on their own terms, in ways that will click. Some of the women need descriptions of a move or trick. Others need an image to think about, and then their bodies will "feel" what to do. Rather than making the athlete or student adjust to the coach, or leader or teacher, it is the leader's responsibility to adjust. Bird and Resnick intuitively adjust to their gymnasts—a useful reminder for the classroom (student-centered learning) and in the business world.

Likewise, Patty Resnick, who is a master choreographer, adjusts the dance moves to the athlete— some are long, fluid, and elegant; others are dynamic, fast, and aggressive. She finds moves and music to fit the strengths of the gymnasts, just like good leaders do in organizations.

So next time you need inspiration about fast decision-making, recruiting, or culture, go see a gymnastics meet.

What Sumo Wrestlers Can Teach Business

February 1, 2016

I was in Japan to visit a friend who I've not seen for twenty years. We met on a plane from Chicago to Tokyo, when I was a young researcher for Battelle on the way to give a speech to two hundred blue-chip Japanese firms. He was the general manager for Sumitomo Metals, North America.

When I wrote him after my conference, he confessed he'd been worried. You had everything going against you, he wrote: "You were young, female, and foreign. I thought your talk would be a disaster."

I ended up doing a research project on professional women who work outside their home countries and started with Japan as the first test case.

I have wanted to visit for a long time, especially since he is aging. On this trip, I stayed with him and his wonderful "new" wife (he was a widower for a year and has now been married again for eighteen years). We talked, ate great food, and went to a Japanese-style hotel where his wife and I visited the hot springs public baths.

We also watched about five hours of a sumo-wrestling tournament on TV.

Now, I admit I wouldn't normally seek sumo wrestling out. But he was interested and was tired from speaking so much English (my Japanese is limited to asking for a cold and delicious beer). As we watched, I tried to figure out what this activity might offer business leaders who are open to learning from four-hundred-pound men, whose work may seem strange to our eyes.

First, you can't avoid global competition. The Japanese are devastated that sumo-wrestling champions have come from outside Japan for the last decade, in a sport that was founded in and dominated for hundreds of years by one country. Right now, the Mongolians, Russians, a Bulgarian, and even a Hawaiian are fierce competitors to the Japanese. But that is motivating to the Japanese right now, not discouraging them.

Second, big bodies can be nimble. Sumo wrestling has a lot to do with timing, leverage, and smarts. Watching these men prepare (eyes-closed meditation, stretching, glaring, and tossing salt) and then move with unexpected speed, balance, and yes, even grace, makes me wonder how big organizations could do the same.

We talk often about remaining nimble, like a small startup. Staying nimble works with a four-hundred-pound man because all of the pieces integrate and work together (mind, heart, and body). How could that happen with a big organization?

The announcers talked about how wrestlers use a "new" grip, or a different face push, or how smaller wrestlers out-leverage larger people. How could businesses do the same?

And last, I appreciated the respect wrestlers show for each other and the sport. Much of the sumo wrestling is ritual: The referee wears a Shinto priest-style garment, the wrestlers hand sacred water in a wooden ladle to one another, they toss purifying salt onto the ring. These actions speak to honor and legacy.

So much of what we do today focuses only on the new, to tossing what was "before." Yet perhaps it's time to review what may have value, to avoid reinventing the wheel, and what needs to be eliminated, rather than just tossing wholesale what has come before. Might work in business. Maybe also in politics.

How Do You Hire for Passion or Curiosity? Here's One Question to Ask

May 9, 2017

When I was a young professor, I invited a very successful entrepreneur to speak to my class. One of the questions was, "How did you learn to hire the right people?"

His response: "I made a lot of mistakes ... on my previous employer's nickel." In other words, he learned how to hire by making loads of bad decisions early in his career. By the time he started his own company, he knew more about what to look for and ask and made fewer mistakes.

Even when people learn through mistakes, it's still a tough call to find the right people, especially when it comes to assessing the less-tangible aspects of job candidates. With the recent talk about how organizational leaders try to find people who "fit" the culture, how do you assess that? How do you know if a person is passionate about your company or industry? What's the way find out if a candidate has innate curiosity that will help her identify new problems or areas to pursue for the company?

I'm about to start a new project and have been reading about how the great interviewers ply their craft. One of the very best is Cal Fussman, who for years wrote a column for Esquire magazine called "What I've Learned." In an interview with HBR.org, Fussman mentioned that many CEOs have approached him to learn how to "find passionate job candidates." As they say, we know how to figure out if a person can do the technical parts of a job, but how can we find out about passion or curiosity?

Fussman told them about an interview he'd done with rapper and entrepreneur Dr. Dre. During the interview, Fussman asked Dr. Dre how long he had gone without sleeping to finish a project he was deeply committed to. The answer, "72 hours."

In essence, Fussman was asking about passion: When a person has the drive, curiosity, and ability to lose himself so much that he forgets to eat or sleep, he's passionate. By asking the sleep question, Fussman got at that question, indirectly but very clearly.

My takeaway is that Fussman suggests asking candidates to talk about times or projects when they have lost track of time and forgotten to eat or sleep because they were so involved or excited about a project. That's having passion, or the drive and curiosity to solve a problem or complete a project.

Fussman's question strikes me as a good one to ask ourselves as well, on a regular basis. Are there occasions that inspire or enthrall us so much we lose track of time? I doubt our whole lives could be that exciting, but are there ways to have more of that in our work or lives and less of the drudgery and mundaneness?

For Leaders, a Slot Canyon Can Provide Perspective on Your Perspectives

May 23, 2017

Last week, I walked into a cool dark strip of sandy space, about 2 feet wide, flanked by high sandstone walls. Snow Canyon Slot in St. George, Utah, was the treat at the end of a long hot hike.

To enter meant squeezing through about a foot of space between a tree trunk and a vertical wall. I made some pretzel body moves—turning sideways, foot extended as far as I could push it, hugging the tree to wriggle myself through. Inside, the air was cool. Petroglyphs covered one side of the fragile sandstone walls. Their makers had a sense of humor, making sheep and humans look almost unworldly in that spooky setting.

But the perspective looking straight up is what struck me: dark walls reaching up 10 times my height. At the top, the contrast with the clear azure sky hurt my eyes. A sliver of moon rested on the edge of the skinny horizon. Then I realized that I could see the moon only because of chance: It happened to be with the range of my slice of view. To see birds or clouds from within that slot would be impossible unless they happened by. The walls gave me a view only directly above. Who would choose that perspective if he or she had a choice to be where the wider landscape was possible?

But that narrow, limited viewpoint is what many of us do choose, almost unwittingly. When we stay within our own fields or disciplines — whether art or engineering, marketing or religion — we are limiting our views. It may not seem so, since there are so many sorts of industries and problems, but in essence we are looking at what happens within the view available, instead of forcing ourselves to seek a wider view.

A day after the slot visit, I hiked up Gunlock Trail. The area around St. George emerged from three major land masses coming together: the Colorado Plateau, the Great Basin and the Mojave Desert. Near the top, the view encompassed bit of each of those, including the Pine Valley laccolith, which is assumed to be the world's largest.

From that vantage, I also saw a cinder-cone volcano and white-checkerboard sandstone, lizards and toads, lichen and moss, narrowleaf yucca and hedgehog cactus. I learned about the interaction of the plants, animals, rocks, water and air.

But my bigger "Aha!" moment was the advantage of having a much wider landscape, which allows me to choose what to look at. I also noticed so many factors beyond my control and thought about how they affected me and I them, if at all.

Leaders need that ability to see a wide view, to expand their perspectives, to realize there are many forces that can influence how their organizations operate. Staying within our own worlds, disciplines, fields and viewpoints will offer us only the odd chance to be exposed to the complexity and wonder of our economic and business opportunities.

My new suggestion on how to expand your perspective: Go take a walk in the Foothills and see what that opens up about your work world.

What Historian David McCullough's New Book Can Teach Idaho Business Leaders

May 30, 2017

I seem to be quoting The Wall Street Journal's Peggy Noonan a lot these days. A few weeks ago, she had an excellent column suggesting that leaders need to think more like artists than economists. This past week she reviewed a collection of speeches by the historian David McCullough, who has much to offer leaders of any type of organization.

McCullough's book, "The American Spirit," argues that history is a "larger way of looking at life." His focus is on how politicians can use history, but I think it can help business leaders too.

Here are some of the keys from McCullough's book that Noonan mentions:

History is a story, about people. I grew up thinking of history as a collection of dates and facts. Historians say, instead, that it explains how and why people behave as they do. I've come to think of it as a layperson's guide to psychology, providing context, actions and consequences that we can learn from without having to live through them. Think about what we've learned by watching Sheryl Sandberg go from a regular business leader to one who inspires women and now, people who grieve.

People in history were living in their own "present," even as we see them in "the past." We live our lives in the present, without the benefit of hindsight (until whatever we do is over). It's the same for historical characters. They were living, deciding and acting in their own "present." Similarly, decisions made today about why, what, and how to educate, compete, or invent can have far reaching impacts. By learning about how historical figures analyzed, considered and then made decisions that had consequences known to us now, perhaps we can be better at informing ourselves before acting.

Nothing is—or was—guaranteed. The actions people in history took were, as I mentioned, in their "present." They could have taken other steps and the results could have been very different. The same holds true today. Leaders typically cannot do an experiment, testing one decision against another, but rather must make decisions in their own way, using what information they choose to assess. Thus, the results of a decision can spin out in a number of ways. Good leaders, of course, do try to consider what those various outcomes could be as they weigh the decisions. But nothing is guaranteed.

History exposes hubris. Arrogance is too often a danger for people in power. History shows us that hubris can lead, ultimately, to an inability to see what's happening in reality. As Shakespeare's King Lear found, giving in to flattery, or being unwilling to listen to bad news, can lead to one's own downfall as well as an organization's, which brings VW or Wells Fargo to mind.

Perhaps one of your summer reads should be a great history book.

When "No Action" Is Better Than "Action?"

June 23, 2015

Creative people know that acting in unexpected ways, including not acting at all, may sometimes be the smartest step to take.

First, with soccer in the news, for reasons both good and bad, it made me remember a research study that suggests not acting can be a good thing. In 2007, Israeli researchers investigated goalkeepers' actions during penalty kicks. They examined three hundred kicks and found that 94 percent of the goalies dove to the side of the goal box, even when their chances of stopping the ball were minimal. In fact, standing still would have given them a greater opportunity to stop the ball.

So why did they act?

The goalkeepers jumped sideways because they wanted to appear as though they were doing something. They were trying to make a difference. Of course, making the game more exciting probably didn't hurt ratings or love for the players. But, according to the researchers, the goalkeepers really had a greater chance of stopping the ball if they had stood still.

A second piece of research also raises the benefits of doing nothing, but in a different way. In 2011, researchers Tillburg and Igou found boredom can lead to a feeling of meaninglessness. And, over time, when people do nothing, they eventually become more interested in finding ways to put meaning into their lives, which then makes them act, sometimes to help others. In essence, doing nothing leads to boredom, which can eventually generate positive behaviors as people search for meaning.

Maybe it's a stretch but perhaps that's what the goalies are doing—by acting, leaping toward the edge of the goal box, they give meaning to their role. Even though standing still is a better option for the desired outcome of stopping the ball, moving and acting may be better for the individual player's sense of meaningfulness.

I knew about the value of using downtime or boredom as a way to trigger the mind to become more creative, but I'd never thought about the value of boredom in helping to generate thoughts of meaningfulness.

So try doing nothing for a while and see what comes. It's summer, after all.

Lessons from a Safari Guide Who Sees "Behind the Trees"

June 20, 2016

I recently spent a couple of weeks in Botswana on a photo safari. There were elephants, lions, bee-eaters, saddle-billed storks, monitor lizards, and baobab trees that expand when they soak up water. Even for a nonzoologist, the safari was nirvana.

One of the best parts, though, was learning from the guides.

On our last night in DumaTau camp, guide Nametsegang (a.k.a. "Name") Dihoro took us on a riverboat ride to watch elephants crossing and see the sunset. As he was giving six of us a lecture on the Okavango Delta area, he stopped midsentence.

"I've never seen this before."

Name rarely shows excitement, because, frankly, over his six years working as a guide, he had seen just about all there was to see. But he was stunned.

He pointed to a pride of fourteen lions walking along the riverbank, heading toward our camp. He radioed the camp's manager so people could get away from the pool, the tents, and the floating dock, since the lions were just a couple of hundred yards away. He took photos and moved closer to the bank for a better look. Five of the lions did go into the camp, walked past our tents and kept on going. The others veered off and headed into the bush.

Name never expected to see lions so close to a major body of water and had never seen so many headed straight for the camp. The rest of us were almost unfazed. (No, we were actually quite happy to be far out in the water, safely away from the lions.) But we had no inkling of how unusual this sighting was until we saw Name's reaction.

Lesson for me: Experts notice in ways different from novices.

Another example made the point even more directly. I asked Name how he finds animals in the bush, especially ones that are camouflaged by the grass and trees.

"I used to think of the grass and trees as a wall, a barrier to seeing animals," he said. "I looked into the trees and couldn't find them. But now I look 'behind' the trees and the grass and see animals all over the place."

As Name described it, he has practiced his skills and reached a point where he sees and senses what's "behind" a tree. He said he had started spending time in the bush as a child and by six to seven years old had gotten good at tracking. Later, as a "guide in training," he shadowed an experienced person for several months.

But it was only when he began spending a lot of time alone in the wilderness—looking, listening, and reflecting on what was around him—that he began to "see" what the rest of us couldn't.

That's a lesson for leaders in business. Perhaps Name's ability is similar to spending "10,000 hours" to hone a skill. But I would also argue if we really listen, "look," and reflect deeply on what we're experiencing or learning in business, we will become better faster at seeing what others might not.

When someone you know, or you, mentions "seeing" something in the environment or a change in customers, be sure to notice. Try to understand how that's happening.

Who knows? You might become a better tracker in the Idaho woods, too.

Business Leaders, What Are Your Lions in the Grass?

June 1, 2016

You can't get much further from Boise than an African safari: Thirty hours in transit with at least twenty-three hours on a plane.

But I always can learn something for business leaders, no matter where I go.

This time, I have lesson from safari guides who know how to find the "hard to see."

I recently spent two weeks in the Okavango Delta of Botswana, in southern Africa. Every day, we spent about eight or nine hours trying to uncover the "science of the wild," as our guide, Spike Mooketsi, called it. He is an expert at finding elephants, Cape buffalo, shy leopards, and rare Roan antelope. But he excels in finding and following lions.

Spike's "territory" covers about 77,000 acres. Imagine the challenge of finding a fourteen-lion pride in a savannah that size, bumping along in a specially outfitted Land Cruiser at five to seven miles an hour.

How does he do it?

He gets lots of help from the inhabitants themselves, starting with the lions' tracks but continuing with signals from other creatures, from birds to giraffes, kudus to warthogs.

Spike starts by reading the "morning newspaper": animal tracks left throughout the night in the dusty sand. Those tracks, if he finds some, can tell how fast (running or sauntering) lions traveled and in which direction, indicating how far away the lions could be. If a track was made around midnight, then insect or small-animal trails may appear on top of it by 6:00 a.m., suggesting the lions are now far from the trail.

He also listens for warning calls from birds, perched high in trees, that can see lions in the grass. He watches giraffes to see if they are all facing a certain direction and on alert. He looks for whether other animals are "out of their routines." He also scouts for unusual patterns, colors, or shapes. He especially looks for movement.

In tall grass, lions seem to disappear. Amazingly, it's hard to see, let alone hear, a five-foot long, three-hundred-pound lion. But if he has read the signs right, Spike will find them.

And there they are: the black backs of their ears, the twitching black tail tips, and the rustling grass around them.

Sounds like what a business leader might need to consider, don't you think?

Watching for the unexpected, finding the hard to see, by reading the signs: warning calls from customers, employees who might seem out of their routines, or odd movements or changes from competitors.

What lions do you need to be on the lookout for? And how do you try to find them?

The Problems with Lawyers' Billable-Hours Business Model

November 19, 2014

I've been thinking about assumptions a lot lately, especially how difficult it is to question the ones we may not even realize we hold. Business-model assumptions are some of the toughest to challenge and to change. But I saw it happened recently when one CEO listened to someone from another industry. That CEO ended up changing his firm's approach to compensation because of challenges to his assumptions.

The company I have in mind provides services to organizations all over the United States, some of which are nonprofits. The firm billed on an hourly basis for its services. That began to cause some concern for several of its customers. They worried that they would be hit with unexpectedly high rates, especially since they couldn't predict what their bills would be.

And as the CEO explained, the system rewarded employees who took longer to get a job done: The more hours they took the more money the firm, and they, could make. Rather than encouraging efficient work, the system encouraged slower processing, costing customers more.

In a meeting with other aggressive learners from outside of his industry, the CEO talked about how frustrating this system was for his anxious customers and unrewarded high-performing employees. Then a lawyer spoke up.

In the traditional law firm, attorneys bill in fifteen-minute chunks. If you have a job you need legal help on, you may not know what your final bill will be, because the lawyers may need more time than anticipated at the start. Still, some projects are fairly routine and should be predictable.

Exactly my situation, said the CEO of the service-provider firm.

Also, said the attorney, given the legal business's focus on "billable hours," lawyers need to show they are working, and they do that by filling up hours.

Exactly my situation, said the CEO.

As the discussion progressed, it became clear the CEO was using the law firm model and that was not working for him. It didn't work for his customers, who wanted predictable prices for jobs they needed to have done. It didn't reward productive employees.

The CEO returned to his company and reorganized its pricing approach so customers would have a fixed rate for certain types of projects and employees would have clearer expectations about what level of output they should be able to achieve in a given length of time.

For several years, the CEO had used a model he thought made sense for his company and industry. He made assumptions that this was the way things had to be done. As problems emerged, he realized he needed to shake things up. When he realized that essentially he had been using a law firm model that didn't work, he changed.

With the likely changes in the legal sector, don't you wonder if law firms are questioning their own business models?

What Can Nonprofits Teach Business

December 17, 2014

After talking to leaders of nonprofit- and profit-making organizations over the years, I wonder if, in some ways, the former may be harder to run than the latter.

Granted, nonprofit leaders don't face quarterly financial goals or upset shareholders at annual meetings, but still, their challenges are vexing. And perhaps, business leaders could get ideas from understanding those challenges.

First, some nonprofit leaders have boards that rotate yearly or biannually; often, that means a new board president. Imagine the flexibility you'd need, having a new boss, with new directions, every single year. That means constant educating of the board, helping members to understand what can, and must not, change.

Next, the types of board members can vary wildly, even as they all support the organization and its mission. Some people join boards to build their resumes. Others are major donors, and may or may not want a say in the organization's future. Still others join as a way for their companies to support the community. Regardless, the nonprofit leader must understand and balance the different types of board members, which demands tact and good negotiating abilities.

Another part of managing nonprofit boards is simply running meetings. Since board members may have very different "day jobs," they may either seek or not worry so much about meeting efficiency. Some members may be executives in their own firms, willing to take time over lunch or breakfast for a board meeting but unable to participate in long discussions. For others, the board may be their work, and if they love it, they may want those meetings to last far longer than the executives anxious to get back to their own organizations.

In addition, nonprofit organizations also typically have many volunteers, sometimes running into the hundreds. The volunteers also will have different reasons for wanting to be part of the organization as well as varying levels of commitment. One of the biggest jobs, then, that nonprofit leaders face is motivating unpaid volunteers, who may feel less obliged to get a job done than if they were paid by the organization.

Lastly, I hear too many nonprofit leaders saying that business leaders want to tell them how to run a nonprofit. Maybe there needs to be more learning in both directions.

So what can business leaders learn from nonprofit leaders?

All of these are points that good leaders should know already, of course, but just to review:

- Be attuned to and learn how to manage your boss(es), all shapes and sizes.
- Be flexible with a changing boss or board, but know when to stand firm.
- Know what drives people and expect it to be different.
- Learn to motivate people without the money lever. This is especially crucial with younger generations.
- Finally, appreciate that we can learn from each other, profit making or not.

Good lessons, no matter what type of organization you run.

How Big Goals Can Tap Unseen Options

October 29, 2015

When did you last go to the zoo in Boise? If your kids are grown, maybe it's been a while. If so, you won't believe how much it's improved. User- and animal-friendly exhibits, lots of people, chances to interact with the animals…but that's only part of it.

Zoo Boise has done something as an organization that makes it a leader among accredited zoos and aquariums by generating lots of money to save animals in the wild. And it stems from thinking big and being able to see something that others don't.

Steve Burns, Zoo Boise's director, tells a remarkable story about how the zoo changed its mission and its actions so that it has generated nearly $2 million for conservation of animals in the wild.

But let's take a step back.

Traditionally, zoos have had a mission of educating and inspiring. They hope that kids will learn about animals and perhaps become zookeepers or biologists, or even work in faraway places on conservation efforts. Maybe the hope was that Bill Gates would go to a zoo as a ten-year-old and then when he became rich, he'd donate millions of dollars. As we say in the business world, that's not really a sustainable business model.

But in 2008, as Steve Burns began seeing depressing numbers on how many animals in the wild were disappearing, he wondered what a small zoo in a remote city could do. The number of lions in the wild, for example, has dropped from four hundred thousand to about thirty thousand in twenty years. In a sense, those animals are zoos' raw material source, and, unlike trees, they were not growing but rather declining. So without the chance to see and learn about those animals, how would future generations know and protect them?

Steve saw an article that sparked an idea: Why not find ways to raise money for conservation efforts?

That meant changing the organization's mission first, though. After much discussion, that's what the board and city leaders did, so now the zoo's mission is to "educate, inspire, and generate funds for conservation of animals in the wild."

Zoo Boise started by creating a "conservation fee" of twenty-five cents in addition to the admission price, and five dollars on an annual membership. All of that incremental money went for conservation efforts. During the years, new projects came up, such as having visitors pay to feed the giraffes or taking a boat ride to see the monkeys. In all, there are half a dozen of these experiences around the zoo that allow visitors to give money to support their favorite animals.

Now the amazing part: Of the 225 accredited zoos and aquariums in North America, Zoo Boise is now one of the leaders in raising funds for conservation.

On average, zoos donate about one percent to two percent of their revenues for saving animals in the wild. Care to guess what percentage of Zoo Boise's revenues go for conservation efforts?

Seventeen percent.

Astounding. Ahead of nearly every zoo in the country—a creative way to do something far beyond the local community and help animals in the wild.

Even if we can't be in the wild, the animals benefit. It came from thinking big, starting small, and seeing an opportunity others missed.

Where could you apply that approach—having a big goal that taps unseen opportunities?

Part 2

Planting Seeds for Creativity and Curiosity

Part 2: Planting Seeds for Creativity and Curiosity considers the notions of farming and farmers as places where "seeds" of creativity or curiosity could grow. In addition, Part 2 taps perspectives and questions that most of us miss or do not even seek, such as neuroscience and geophysics, encouraging the idea that knowledge can come from almost anyplace.

Sow Idea Seeds by Preparing Soil, Then Letting Them Grow

July 16, 2014

I'm not a real farmer, or goodness, even a gardener. I've tried to plant tomatoes (disaster) and even roped my family into planting one hundred tulips bulbs one Thanksgiving weekend. All that came of it was happy squirrels and two tulips. But oh, what beautiful tulips they are!

But I consider myself a farmer of a different sort. I plant seeds of ideas.

And to do that, I suspect a few principles that are used by real farmers and gardeners apply for ideas as well.

Prepare the Soil

The environment, or soil, has to be ready to receive the seed of an idea. That means reading an organization and people within it to see if they may be primed for a new idea: Are they beginning to talk about something that is similar? Are they seeking something new to work on or a new way to solve a problem? Is there fear that a competitor is moving ahead? In other words, is the timing right?

Drop Micro Seeds

Next comes a slow process of dropping micro seeds, hints really, that are almost invisible, just to get some of the words or thoughts in the air. That means mentioning something in small ways many, many times (I had no idea how many times until I started tracking this process) and to do it in ways that are not threatening or pushing the idea but rather just tossing it out and seeing what happens.

Cover Your Tracks and Let Someone Else Take the Credit

When we come up with ideas, we believe in them, fight for them, and make them happen. So helping a good idea become someone else's can strengthen it and take it in new and often better directions. Then play the supporter—no longer the initiator—of the idea. That means being ready with a bit more information when needed and being able to support the changes that improve the idea.

Let It Go When It's Time

Fields need to rest, sometimes to prepare for new seeds in the future, sometimes to shift crops or uses altogether; same thing with ideas. Good gardeners—and idea planters—need to let go of an idea and move to the next phase at times.

Long ago, a colleague and I had the world's best idea for our university, or so we thought. While we were trying to persuade our colleagues inside the university to move on the idea, I mentioned it to colleagues elsewhere. Boom! Another college implemented the same idea within a year, while we let it die on the vine. I was ticked but learned two things: First, timing is critical. We weren't ready for the idea and the other university was. Second, you can always generate new ideas. So don't worry about ones that don't work. Let them go.

I've tried to become a better planter—and reaper—of ideas. What seeds could you plant today?

Stealth Creativity

January 29, 2015

A very brave person gave me a holiday gift that could have led to disaster. She knows that I'm an awful gardener: I've tried growing tomatoes half a dozen times over the years and always fail. The two plants in my house live only because someone else kindly remembers to water them. So, in mid-December, I was taken aback when she handed me a square glass container, half filled with beautiful stones and two narcissus bulbs.

"Just cover the stones with water and leave it alone."

Now that's my kind of plant.

So I put it alongside the bathtub and added water. Every day since, it has made its own magic. The shoots were two inches high before I noticed them, and the next day they were at least three. By New Year's, the green stalks were a foot tall, and tiny white flowers were blossoming. For a few days then, the stalks tilted and then bent over. I moved the container closer to the wall to prop them up.

By middle of January, the narcissus had an attitude. It was standing straight, acting like a "I can take it from here" kind of plant. It's solid, it's gorgeous, and I worry that it will bash through the ceiling. The plant seemed to find its own way to thrive, in part because of what I did *not* do. Yes, I gave it water and a protected environment, but mostly left it alone to see what would happen.

For me, ideas are like small bulbs or seedlings at their birth. They sit there like funny ducklings, often ugly and with little to endear themselves. But a good leader—or any of us hoping to have ideas—needs to do what I did with the narcissus: give ideas a little air and water, avoid stepping (or stomping) on them and often, they'll just work their way to becoming stronger, stand-alone types of ideas. And then, if you're lucky and treat them right, they may blossom into something gorgeous and better yet, useful.

Often the best chance that ideas have—like my tiny narcissus—is to be somewhere out of the mainstream. Then, they can grow in a stealthy way, with few people aware of them. That was the idea behind the original Skunkworks, which started during World War II when a group of Lockheed engineers began to work on a much-needed airframe for a new engine. The group worked separately from other groups, *off the radar*, and even had no official government contract until the work was finished.

Without the spotlight of expectations, without the pressure to perform, groups that use stealth creativity often are able to give those tiny, weak ideas the time and nurturing they need to grow into something more strong and useful. And what can leaders who understand the value of stealth creativity do to help? Give good ideas, and the people nurturing them, a little breathing space and time, and then, leave them alone. You never know what might blossom that is beautiful.

Why I Think of Myself as a Farmer

July 15, 2015

I walked into an office building the other day when a man in his forties, with a shaved head and an open face, came up to me in the lobby.

"You don't remember me, do you?"

I hate it when people—usually former students—do that. I'm sure my face looked as blank as my mind was.

"You probably hate it when students do that to you."

Yes indeed.

"I was in your introduction to business class that you taught with Kevin Learned."

We taught that one year, in 1994, so we're talking more than twenty years ago.

"I remember the classroom, where I sat, the speakers, the topics. I was an information systems major, and that was when we had to take business classes. So I took yours."

He brought me up to date on the last twenty-plus years of his career, how he has moved up and does work for a firm he loves.

After several decades of teaching, I have probably had thousands of students, and it's always nice to hear from one of them, even if I don't recall the face or name.

And that's why I think of myself as a farmer.

If you know me, you would scoff at the idea. I am a town slicker (not city) of the first order. I am not much of a *get down in the dirt* type. I can't even get tomatoes to grow in my yard. The crocuses, daffodils, and tulips I planted one Thanksgiving weekend never came up.

But I really love it when someone else can get plants going, and I can reap the benefits. Trees we had planted twenty years ago now provide perfect shade from the heat on our deck. I love raspberries in season or mint when I smell it.

In my imagination, I see farming as a process of planting a seed, creating the right environment and conditions so that it will sprout, and nurturing the small plant enough but not too much. I suspect that key to all of this is patience and knowing when to cut away parts that may hurt the bigger gain. Finally, I wonder if a farmer needs to know when to let go and cut it off, once a plant or vegetable is strong—or tasty—enough.

While I don't know much about sowing seeds in the earth, I do know something about planting seeds in minds, which is farming of a different sort. I do the best I can to plant a seed, create good conditions, and hope it takes. Sometimes, I wonder if those idea seeds were actually planted, since it feels like the wind—or other distractions—carries them away.

So it is a pleasant surprise when I run into someone who has used those seeds to build a good career and life.

Then I imagine I'm a farmer, inspired to put in the work and plant more seeds.

I just need to get better at names.

Build a Permeable Organization Where Ideas Flow Easily

May 21, 2014

Years ago, I got interested in a tiny bit of geophysics. I was the outside observer of a PhD dissertation defense. That means I kept the time clock and made sure the professors who were grilling the student didn't browbeat him or her too much. I understood the first hour of the presentation about bore holes and Fresnel waves and then, when they all spoke in math on the whiteboard, I zoned out. But before I did, I realized I'd learned something that could be useful for organizational leaders.

It turns out that two concepts in geology—porosity and permeability—may give leaders a way to understand how ideas may spread, or be hindered from spreading, throughout their organizations. Because I'm not a geologist and always need to think in very simple English, not math, I'll do the same here.

When the ground below us is porous, it has a lot of pockets or holes in it. Those pockets could be filled with water or air or oil or gas or something else. In a porous setting, though, the air or gas or water just sits in the pockets, and doesn't move from the pockets.

Permeability means that those pockets or holes underground are connected so that the water or gas or air can move or permeate from pocket to pocket. The greater or larger those connection pathways, the greater the flow of oil or water or whatever you've got in the pockets.

Now I'm not exactly sure what the benefits of porosity and permeability for geology may be, I can imagine but wouldn't dare to speculate out loud at this point, but I can certainly see benefits of those concepts within an organization.

Many leaders talk about wanting an innovative culture, meaning they want ideas to grow and spread and be useful for the organization. So imagine your organization in our two favorite new geology terms. How porous and permeable is it? You may have pockets of ideas in lots of places, good porosity, but can they flow from unit to unit? If so, that means the permeability of ideas is good and ideas should be able to spread throughout the organization.

If you have low porosity, then you'd not have many pockets of ideas, which could really stump your innovative culture. And if those ideas and the people who have them are not spreading throughout the organization, that low permeability could also curtail chances for creativity and innovation to spread.

So next time you fret that your organization isn't generating new ideas or that *silos* are keeping them from moving around the organization, go outside and look at the ground, and think about porosity and permeability. Then go back to the organization and start digging.

Neurons, Highways, and Creativity

May 31, 2014

Just before driving from McCall to Boise one day, I was reading *Science* magazine. It's one of my favorites, because the first half is written in such a way that science groupies like me can understand what's new in science. The magazine offers low-key, easy-to-understand teasers on research that has just come out. The second half of the magazine contains those actual research articles written by astronomers, neuroscientists, geophysicists, and the like.

When I was skimming a recent issue (April 18, 2014), I stopped at the "easier to read version" about a recent study. It made me think about the drive I had before me, and ultimately about how to be more creative.

A National Institutes of Health researcher, R. Douglas Field, studies myelin, long considered the key insulator of neuronal axons (I would use the word neurons because I can remember it, but I suspect axon is more accurate). As he reports, myelin changes how neural impulses or information flows in the brain. The assumption has been that when neural axons are coated with myelin, the information they transmit moves faster and more efficiently. So scientists have assumed it's a good thing for myelin to cover the full length of a neuron. Damage to myelin can affect the nervous system and lead to conditions like multiple sclerosis, cerebral palsy, or stroke.

Fields found that in some mouse brains, some parts of neuronal axons were uncovered. They had no myelin around them. Further, the mice did not exhibit any of the problems assumed to happen when axons were "unmyelinated." Instead, his research suggests that those uncovered stretches might have a purpose: to allow for more neuron connections to occur, which could mean a stronger brain in other ways. In plain words, his findings raise a question of whether myelin is an "all-or-none" condition or whether the situation and environment may determine when it's necessary.

What does this have to do with highways or creativity?

When I drive on an interstate, it's like having myelin on a neuron—it's a type of insulated experience: I can go faster and more efficiently to my destination.

When I drive the smaller roads, with more intersections and turnoffs, less insulation, I have a chance to see new stretches of landscape. Taking the smaller, less-insulated roads is less efficient, but it could lead to some interesting new knowledge and experiences.

And that's often what we need to become more creative: the chance to get distracted, lost, to find new potential connections, rather than simply to go the fastest and most efficient route to a destination.

It is a question of when to take the insulated-speedy path to a destination or when to take a slower, less-insulated but more open pathway that could generate new connections and ideas.

Desperately Seeking Curiosity

November 17, 2014

Winter is starting early in Boise. With six inches of snow on the ground and more coming, it's a great time to stay in, drink tea, and think about curiosity. The reason snow sparks it is because of a summer experience that brings me full circle.

We had visitors from Vietnam in Idaho last summer—good friends with their two daughters, ages sixteen and eleven. Driving to Stanley brought us past windy, steep hillsides. On one, there was a dirty, hard-packed but very obvious snow bank. The younger daughter, Ha My, squealed and insisted we stop. She wanted "to touch snow." She'd been saying she wanted to touch snow for an hour, so we were all relieved it was finally going to happen.

Scrambling down the ditch by the road and then up the steep wall of ice, we reached out to scrape off a bit of dirty snow and crunch it in our hands. Ha My was ecstatic. Why was she so interested?

"I've heard about snow," she said. "I've read about snow. I know other people who touched snow. But I never did. Now I touched snow!"

And that brings me to curiosity.

I just read a fascinating book, *Curious*, by Ian Leslie. He could have been writing about Ha My. Apparently, curiosity is shaped like an inverted *U* curve: You need to know *something* about a topic to be curious, but if you know "too much," you'll think you don't need to ask questions or learn anything more. My young friend exemplified that exact situation: She knew a bit about snow but not too much, so she was curious to learn more.

That reminded me of a very odd evening I spent years ago with a person who was fascinated by numismatics, the study of coins.

Yawn.

But that man had such an enthusiasm and ability to reel me in that for about an hour I was ready to become the world's biggest collector. I didn't. But I remembered that feeling of being curious enough to want more. It was heavenly.

Think about that in your own life. How often do you feel that zing of curiosity and learning something new? How often do you feel bored or that you "know enough already" and thus don't ask questions, don't look at something in a new way or tap that curiosity we all do have in us, just waiting for a trigger?

The thrill we heard in that young person's voice, as we watched her hands waving in front of her as she jumped up and down in excitement at snow, was marvelous. It's even more fun to feel that ourselves. And what a useful skill to have in our work worlds.

So here's a challenge: Learn a little about something new. Listen to a friend, read an article, and watch a program. See what that sparks. And in the meantime, what can you learn about snow?

Can You Have Too Much Stimulation?

August 13, 2015

On a recent visit to the Los Angeles area, I think I had too much stimulation. I'm embarrassed to admit it, since I know that to be creative, different inputs and stimulation are critical, but in this case, I was overwhelmed.

In less than three days, I visited what felt like six totally different cultures and spent about seven hours in traffic, which feels like a culture unto itself. I went to a one-hour production of *Midsummer Night's Dream* at Zombie Joe's theater in NoHo, North Hollywood, pretended I was a Great Gatsby extra at the opulent gardens and houses of the Huntington Galleries, zipped along on the superwide, supermanicured interstates of Orange County, and saw lots of skin, plain, and inked, on Venice Beach. I even had a run-in with a man who may have thought I stole his soul with my camera.

"You pointed your camera in my direction. You cannot. Erase that photo. Now."

"I will, I will."

"Not will. Do it now. I must see."

Geeee whiz.

To be creative, it's important to get new input, but is it possible to have too much coming in? And why does it feel that way?

Three reasons:

First, for me, everything seemed "new" in Los Angeles, and I couldn't process it fast enough. From the intricate graffiti on the buildings to cars racing along the freeway shoulder before zipping into line to the range of footwear (at least 70 percent of all people wear flip-flops, but oh, what a variety), I looked up and down and close and far away. I had FOMO—fear of missing out—and couldn't not look.

Second, the place engaged my senses, fully. I've always thought of Boise as a bit antiseptic—the air is clear and clean, usually, so we don't have the scents that other places do, from food to people, plants to pollution. Idaho is dry, so I don't "feel" the air, but in Los Angeles, humid heaviness weighted down my arms. Los Angeles restaurant noise was enough to make conversation a strain and yet the languages, many I couldn't identify, and topics at the nearby tables fascinated me.

And third, the switch factor—going from one culture to another so quickly—was harder than I expected. I've traveled a fair amount. Even compared to Europe, where cultures and languages are close to each other, Los Angeles's diversity stands out: fun, stimulating, and exhausting.

The key, I suspect, is finding the kind of stimulation that works for you. For some people, big cities do the trick. For others, it's nature.

So what works for you?

To find out, be more methodical in noticing when creativity happens. What conditions, what types of stimulation seem to help—or hinder—the flow? See if you can identify when you had *Aha!* moments for solving problems or finding new ideas. Who knows, it might even be in traffic!

Leave It to the Farmers to Get It Done

July 13, 2016

I'm an eclectic reader. When I'm in an airport, I'll buy magazines I never would normally read—from wrestling or organic farming to hang gliding or horses.

They give me ideas that might be useful for business or the rest of my life. Then I bump into other articles, and often they all connect.

I looked at an old issue of *Science* magazine (November 28, 2014) with an interview of an MIT professor that sparked some thoughts. Robert S. Langer talked about connections between science and entrepreneurship. One quote stood out:

"When you're a student, you're judged by how well you answer questions. But in life, you're judged by how good your questions are."

Sounds like the perfect characteristic of an entrepreneur.

Then, I stumbled onto a May 2, 2016, *Wall Street Journal* article about how a thirty-year-old Matt Reimer from Manitoba used coursework from the MIT website and online forums to create a robot tractor from drone parts and open-source software. Reimer claims the tractor helped save him $8,000 last year, equivalent to part of the pay for a tractor driver.

What's remarkable is that this young farmer, who dropped out of engineering school, likely exemplifies the future of farming entrepreneurship. He knew what questions to ask and went about finding a solution.

We talk about making America great as if we've lost it all. (Then again, Canada may already be great with folks like Reimer inventing cool equipment.) But we have so much of what has already made us great: ingenuity, innovation, and drive to solve a problem. As Reimer told the *WSJ*, even if autonomous tractors come out next year, it would be "fifteen years before that technology trickles down to every farm." Why wait? He just got it done.

So rather than listening to bombast, I'm putting my money on the ability of people who actually do the work—in the field, on the factory floor, in the classroom or the operating room—to ask good questions and find ways to do things differently to get better. Just get it done.

Part 3

Brainstorming New Ideas

Part III: Brainstorming New Ideas offers up ways to help leaders generate ideas, especially from outside of their industries, but also from outside the United States. Even industries that might seem old-fashioned or "set" have opportunities to find new ways to operate.

An App to Find Clean Restrooms Nearby? Let's Get It Here

February 29, 2016

I frequently scan future-oriented websites for new or unusual ideas that might be emerging. Often, the most interesting ones come from rather far-off places.

Trendwatching.com's September report on the future of digital consumerism in Asia had a number of great ideas, some of which might be interesting to develop in the United States. Here are just a few that I certainly would love to have:

Thai-based Parking Duck is a shared site where home and office owners can post and then rent out empty parking spaces in real time. It's a sort of Airbnb for cars. If your firm has unused capacity, just put it on the open market (in this case Parking Duck). Does an equivalent idea exist for restaurants that would have open slots in fifteen minutes on a Friday night when I decide to go out (and I don't have a reservation)?

Another phone app, GottaGo, comes out of India and does just what you imagine it might: It provides a list of over 10,000 clean restrooms in several cities in India based upon your location. Now wouldn't that be useful in most American cities or even on the road?

Asiri Group of Hospitals, based in Sri Lanka, created the "Soap Bus Ticket." Buses sell tickets that are permeated with soap, so riders can use their disposable tickets to clean their hands and, ultimately, reduce the spread of germs. In what other settings might a cleanser be applied?

A final example is from India again. Khushi offers a "smart necklace" with vaccination records on a chip that health providers scan. Babies wear the necklaces, saving their parents needing to carry a paper copy.

While these are intriguing ideas in themselves, my bigger point is to scour many sources for new ideas—or possible threats to our products or services. So start scheming: what would you use?

It's Time to Bring Back Medical House Calls

March 14, 2016

No one would think me athletic, but I did once sprain my ankle in a basketball game. Maybe that's when I decided to quit playing any sport.

That day, in PE class, I jumped up and landed in an ungraceful way on my right foot, ankle bone on the floor. I hobbled home. My mother phoned our family doctor, who was also a family friend. He stopped by on the way home from work, checked my ankle, and had a beer with my dad.

I thought about Dr. V again as I was reading Well+Good's projection of trends in 2016 that relate to health.

One category referred to the "uberization" of health and beauty services. Apparently in large cities, you can get a massage, a facial, or a manicure "delivered" to your door, home or office, in moments. Zeel is an app that allows for requesting same-day, in-home massages. The Ritualist is for facials, and Manicube offers manicures at your desk. Other sites offer drop-in services, sort of like the XpresSpa idea at airports. You just stop in, have a fifteen-minute massage and go on your way. The rationale is that busy people want convenience, a little bit of luxury, and supposedly to do something good for their health, and they often want it at home.

That's why I remember Dr. V and started to wonder: Are we perhaps headed back to a world of home visits by medical professionals?

We have express drop-in medical outlets in grocery stores and on the street corner. When will we have in-home delivery of medical care?

I doubt I'll see my family doctor swing by my house on the way home, although I'd be happy to offer him a beer, but with so many more options for health care providers, could others step in?

One friend has arranged for a physician's assistant to do regular checkups on her aging mother in her assisted-living residence. Why not house calls for the rest of us?

Let Others' Green-Tech Ideas Ease You into a Creative State

March 18, 2015

Creativity scares some people who say "I don't have good new ideas."

So I say: Start with someone else's idea and see what you can build on.

Green technologies offer a great starting point.

I went looking for cool green technologies to practice generating different ideas.

A site called Mother Nature Network, mnn.com, was a treasure trove. Here are a few of the wackier ideas, still in progress, that give a chance to practice creativity and see just what else can come from a good starting idea.

Pencil Printer

Have you ever had a no. 2 pencil stub that you almost can't use but still has a little lead in it? You poke the eraser end into your palm and write just a bit longer to get full use. Enter the "pencil printer," by Yanko Design (yankodesign.com). It strips the wood from nearly used-up pencils and converts the leftover lead to printer ink. An interesting way to get full benefit from the pencil. Next step: Wouldn't it be great if Yanko could transform the leftover pencil wood to create printer paper?

River Gym

In 2005, *New York* magazine held a contest asking designers to rethink gyms. Mitchell Joachim and Douglas Joachim (inhabitat.com) developed the human-powered "River Gym" on a boat. The floating gym captures energy that people generate during their workouts—from stationary bicycles, elliptical machines, or rowing machines—to power the boat crossing a river. Not only that, but the floating gym includes a process to clean the water. The hard-working exercisers get a great river view—and would feel plenty smug, I suspect.

We don't need to power boats in Boise, but what about using workout energy to run building elevators or office lights?

Or: Is there a way to capture the foot power of students walking across campus sidewalks?

How else might we capture already-generated energy for use elsewhere?

Moss Carpet

Love the feeling of soft green plants under your bare feet? Why not take that feeling to your bathroom?

Designer Nguyen La Chanh (also at inhabitat.com) created "moss carpet" that sits in a recycled latex foam container. Put it right next to your shower or bathtub. When you step in or out, you wiggle your toes on a soft green surface. Because moss thrives in moist dark places, the bathroom is perfect.

The idea got me wondering about growing walls of moss or plants. Could they help generate a calm setting and clean the air a bit while they're at it? Or: Could I put favorite fragrances into the moss, like lavender or bergamot? As I step on the moss, a little whoosh of scent could come out. A nice way to start my day.

Generating ideas is great fun once you get over the fear of sounding strange. So why not start with someone else's odd idea and build on that?

It's good practice, and you may come up with some great products along the way.

Student's Innovation That Benefits Old and Young Alike

February 18, 2015

When I was first married, I made spaghetti one night. Mind you, I never learned to cook when I was growing up, because my mother was the world's best cook. She did it better than anyone in the family and was protective of her kitchen. So when I found the person I would marry and discovered that he was a great cook, I was over the moon.

Still, as a newlywed, I felt guilty not cooking, so I tried. Hence, the night Nancy cooked spaghetti.

The problem was, of course, that not knowing much about cooking meant I didn't know much about cutting and chopping. Very soon, there was an unintended ingredient in the spaghetti sauce, just a dash of blood. I confessed, covered my finger with a Band-Aid and handed over the knives. Needless to say, I've not been the go-to chef when it comes to serious chopping.

I recently began wondering about who invented the Band-Aid. Apparently, it was Earle Dickson, an employee of Johnson & Johnson in the 1920s. He created the first Band-Aid for his wife, who tended to slice her fingers when she was cooking. Thank you, Ms. Dickson, for making that mistake. Thank you, Mr. Dickson, for fixing it and creating something we can't live without.

That process of invention, where someone notices a problem that people face and try to fix it, goes on in most fields, of course. When it comes to health and aging, in particular, it seems we're entering a boom period of invention, thanks to designs schools, organizations like Aging2.0, a network of innovators working in the fifty-plus market, and Stanford's Center on Longevity.

Each year, Aging2.0 and the Stanford center challenge university students around the world to come up with inventions that will improve the lives of older people. The latest challenge focused on ways to enhance mobility.

The finalists are now out. They range from a sensor-based lighting system that helps people move around in their homes at night to a video-based exercise program that allows people to "exercise together" when they are physically apart, and to a tool that helps people get up after they fall so they don't need to call another person for help.

What inspires me is that such a project achieves several outcomes. It supports the notion of generating new business ideas and companies, which is something we are trying to do in Boise as well. It alerts younger people to what life is like for older people, which I hope, increases their empathy for the issues we'll all face. Also, maybe it sparks relationships between the generations, which is hard as we become so mobile and so connected through technology rather than through face-to-face contact.

And finally, design thinking, which is core to this process, demands that inventors interact with users. So again, young people had to interact with and learn about the worlds of others they may not know well.

Sort of "bridging generations for good."

Banking Creativity—on the Way for Idaho?

August 17, 2015

When I worked in Vietnam in the 1990s, we went to the bank monthly to get cash to pay for rent and salaries of the people working on our capacity building project. A colleague and I went to an international bank— ANZ—to take out $30,000 worth of local currency. In those days, the denominations went no higher than the equivalent of a five dollars bill, so we carried the cash out of the bank in four white plastic bags, with "ANZ" in big black letters on the side. Then we'd sit, $30,000 at our feet, and eat lunch before heading to the office.

How things change.

I was in Hanoi recently and, as in the rest of the world, ATMs, international transfers, and mobile banking are common. But I just read about another bank—ING—and its use of technology, and I'm fascinated to see when we will catch up in the United States.

In the August 2 issue of the *Financial Times*, a profile of the CEO of Amsterdam-based ING bank mentioned several whiz-bang sounding technologies.

Ralph Hamers visited Silicon Valley to learn what his bank might incorporate and found the techies interested in learning from him. As he says, banking products are all alike. A mortgage or bank account is the same no matter where you go. What will differentiate is how the customers receive and experience service.

Here are four ways he's beefed up the bank's service using technology—some, of course, make visiting the bank obsolete altogether:

- In Spain, ING is piloting an "algorithmic credit scoring system" that sounds like the one used by organizations like Kiva.org, where peers lend to small firms without any direct interaction.

- In Germany, the bank won authority to open bank accounts using video and face-recognition technology, eliminating the need for face-to-face contact. Now, that fingerprint identification is available on smart phones, and ING has moved to use it in some mobile banking applications.

- The last two involve how people work. In the headquarters office, ING has redesigned its ground floor to be more imaginative. It's now a laboratory with beanbags, white boards, and swing chairs.

- And instead of silos, the bank throws employees from different areas together on a problem or activity, using principles of the software approach called "scrum."

Granted, some employees have lost the traditional jobs, but would these approaches open up some new avenues and ways to work?

Who's going to be first in our market to try some of these new approaches? If it doesn't happen here soon, I'll look for it in Vietnam.

A Drone for House Hunting?
Rethinking Real-Estate Sales

April 15, 2015

A colleague was excited to tell me last week about his stay at a very cool hotel called citizenM, right by the Paris airport. He said, "It's like they redesigned the whole hotel experience, from the ground up."

He's right. the citizenM hotel group has developed an affordable, convenient luxury experience. You check yourself in and out, beds and bathrooms are very high-end, hot food is available twenty-four hours a day, and they hire people without hotel experience and then train them the citizenM way. All this for seventy-nine dollars/night at the hotel in Paris. As the owners say, people want efficiency, emotion, and a great experience, at an affordable price.

That got me wondering about what the residential real-estate experience would be like if Realtors rethought it "from the ground up," in terms of what I might define as a "great experience" buying a house.

So, with apologies to the experts, I do this a lot, here are two, perhaps wacky, ideas that might appeal to someone like me, or my demographic. And yes, I know these would be hard to implement. But I'm in the brainstorming mode now.

First, I'd like a drone that I could maneuver inside and outside of a house I'm considering as a potential buyer. The drone would be soft-sided, of course, so it wouldn't damage walls when it bumps into them. But having a sort of "on call" drone would allow me to look at the places in a house I'm especially interested in, at a pace I want, without depending upon someone physically meeting me to let me inside. I could "visit" the house and the neighborhood at different times of day, instead of driving around at nine o'clock at night to see how noisy it is. It would also save me time and gasoline and make the process a bit more private, more efficient, and less emotional.

Next, could there be real-estate packages tailored to different demographic groups? A "family with small kids" package or an "empty nester" package?

I'd be in the latter category. If I had a wish list, and a lot of money, I'd want an experience that makes my move painless. That would include selling my old house, buying the new place, after using the drone to look at several, and a teleport type of moving experience, where the setup in my current living room (or bedroom, or whatever) is essentially replicated in the new place (with pictures in generally the same positions, silverware in generally the same position in the kitchen, and so on). If the "teleporter movers" could put my house to order, or at least 75 percent of it, that would make the idea of a move so much less stressful.

My point here, obviously, is simply to ask: What would a rethink of an industry look like? We've seen it elsewhere—Uber, Airbnb, citizenM hotel. Why not in real estate?

Envision a World of Drive-Through Payments and One-Card Shopping

August 21, 2016

Many years ago, on the way to do an executive training session in Sun Valley, I stopped to get gas. I spilled gasoline on my shoes and skirt. Since I didn't have time to change clothes, when I arrived at the training program, I didn't smell especially fetching. I was terrified that someone would light a cigarette nearby and I'd burst into flames. Perhaps a dramatic training course gimmick, but not one I wanted to test.

I've hated pumping gas ever since. My good husband does it for me 90 percent of the time. I used to go to a full-serve station on Hill Road in Boise to avoid pumping it myself, but now that's gone. So I have always been on the lookout for easier ways to get some tasks, like tank filling, done. I don't expect gas-tank fills to go automatic anytime soon, but I still began thinking about other ways to shop and pay.

Last year, I discovered that the car wash I go to had a "pay a monthly fee and come in as often as you like" program. Now, when I drive up, the tag on my car alerts the system that I'm a frequent washer, the arm lifts, and away I go. One minute later, I'm done and on my way. It is sort of like the E-Z Pass system on tunnels and toll roads around the country.

So why aren't more organizations—and their banking partners—finding ways to use such drive-through automatic-pay technology?

I read about Apple Pay, where you use your phone to pay, and Apple's collaboration with McDonald's to use Apple Pay there. Another system out of Russia was even more intriguing: a patented drive-through grocery store.

A customer drives past a rotating shelf, scrolls through available items and chooses what she wants, places them on a conveyor belt, and a cashier checks her out.

So I began speculating about other places where you could have your payment deducted automatically, without having to present a card each time. Could we build in E-Z Pass-type payment into a credit or debit card that you add services to when you sign up? You could avoid stuffing so many cards in your wallet, because the pay system would read when you have it and just let you through (or deduct payment). You could add places to the card as you joined them—the art museum, the zoo, your bank safety deposit "key"—and your "do it all" smart card would keep track of it all for you, sitting in your pocket.

I suppose the next step is the implant you could "add to" on demand. But I'm a wimp when it comes to needles, so I'll pass on that.

Part 4

Getting Better

Part 4: Getting Better provides a few final tips for business leaders to carry out their jobs in more efficient and creative ways. Many of these ideas are ones we know but just need to be reminded to do, now and then.

I Need to Block out Distractions to Focus on a Task. You Do, Too

September 29, 2016

I used to cringe when my high-school-age son disappeared under headphones to do homework. Likewise, at many work places, millennials insist they can multitask when they listen to music while working.

I'm the opposite. I need quiet, a space apart from the world, and no distractions if I am going to write, read, or concentrate on something.

But recently, I have begun to wonder if we're not all more the same than I realized.

A recent podcast and some new workplace research reporting on the negative aspects of open offices suggest that most people actually do need "space" to focus, when they are doing brain work. So perhaps they learn to manage the process in different ways.

Malcolm Gladwell, of *The Tipping Point* and *Outliers* fame, recently did an interview with Tim Ferris. In his podcasts, Ferris interviews high performers from different fields and, as he says, "deconstructs" their habits and methods of being productive. His questions range from "What do you do for the first hour of your day?" to "What book do you give most to other people?"

Gladwell, who worked at the *Washington Post* and at the *New Yorker* before going out on his own to write bestselling nonfiction books, is a prolific writer. So, of course, Ferris asked him whether he ever has writer's block.

Gladwell said that working for a newspaper does not allow for writer's block, so he never had it. You can't go to an editor and say, "It's just not working for me right now," when there's a deadline in an hour. In fact,

Gladwell now spends the first half of his day in a coffee shop, writing.

How does he concentrate? Again, he talks about his newspaper days, when noise, talking, and chaos were all around him (unlike today, he says, where the newsrooms are not so loud). So his lesson is: Find a way to focus even when things are noisy around you.

I saw an example of that focused concentration in my university's College of Business and Economics building the other day. The lobby is a sunny two-story room, with a coffee shop, comfortable chairs, and lots of places to work and chat. About twenty-five people sat in pairs or alone, and all but two were on some electronic device. They were completely engaged, writing, or reading (now, to be honest, I didn't look to see if some were playing video games. I don't want to spoil my image of hard-working students).

Their stillness, lack of fidgeting, and intense looks certainly gave the impression that even when people say they are multitasking, they may not be: they are focused and able to block distracting input.

So I have a new challenge: how to be more focused in the midst of commotion. I'll have lots of opportunity to practice. I'm about to take an overseas trip, passing through lots of airports and noise. Focus, here I come.

On Being Magnanimous—a New Route to Creativity?

December 15, 2016

What happens when an organization that has long struggled to have enough money for regular operations—say, a nonprofit—finally reaches a stage where donations and revenue-generating activities thrive?

Instead of constantly saying "no" to employees' requests for funding to try a new program, the director can say "yes."

One such director says this situation has allowed him to have a "magnanimous mindset."

A Treasure Valley nonprofit hired this director several years ago. His task was ominous: to bring the organization back into the black financially, to find ways to increase its visibility both locally and nationally, and to raise the caliber and quality of its offerings. The director reckoned he would need five to seven years to reach those goals. So he was delighted when the organization achieved them all in a much shorter timeframe.

The organization now has enough money to operate without fear of insolvency, it has been consistently rated as one of the best of its kind in the U.S., and the product quality has skyrocketed. He asked that he and his organization not be named, because the nonprofit still needs donations and he doesn't want donors to stop because its finances have improved.

While the improvements have eased the apprehensions of both director and staff, the director began to notice something else: He and the others discovered they could be more creative.

Many people say innovation and creativity come from "necessity" or "being hungry." True, in some ways. If you need to solve a serious problem and are forced by resources or timeline, many groups are very able to step up. Think of the rescue of the Apollo 13 astronauts.

But if we are always starving, desperate to stay alive — as a person or an organization — could that also have dampening effect, leading to solving just immediate problems, rather than having any chance for finding new opportunities?

By having more resources, the director found he could say "yes" to creative new ideas that employees have. He and they could pursue opportunities for even more exciting projects than they had imagined.

Every request or opportunity still needs to support the mission of the organization, of course, but now employees can dream a bit. By having a few extra resources, the director can "be magnanimous" and ultimately even more creative.

Leaders Must Be More Like Artists, Less Like Economists

April 3, 2017

I understand that in the olden days, when people read print newspapers, many readers had favorite columnists. I buy that idea and even now, I have a few that I look forward to reading — both online and in print — because of their ideas, their writing styles, or the way they rile me (in good and bad ways).

One of my favorites is a staunch Republican who writes for The Wall Street Journal and came to fame many years ago as a speechwriter for Ronald Reagan.

Peggy Noonan writes a column for the Saturday edition of the WSJ and, more times than not, it's a kick to read. She clearly leans one direction, but she also tries to be fair to opposition politicians.

What I enjoy most is the way she conceptualizes an idea.

She had a zinger for me recently when she analyzed the Republican party leadership.

Let's just say she's disappointed. The GOP leadership today reminds her of an observation "that a great leader has more in common with an artist than an economist. Economists drill deep in narrow fields, but the artist's view is more expansive; he's more able to grasp the big picture and see how it is changing."

She goes on to say the GOP leadership needs a "greater artistic sense" and maybe "they can put in for a grant from the NEA before it's too late."

That notion of thinking like an artist versus an economist is what grabbed me. Yes, we need people who can dig deeply into specific issues and problems (we have Nobel prizes for those folks), but in complex times with complex problems, leaders need to be able to see a larger landscape. So many challenges demand many perspectives, and that's what artists do naturally.

An artist friend explained once that you should look at a painting from at least three perspectives: from 4 inches away, from 4 feet away and from 40 feet away. At each standpoint, the view is somewhat different, and together they make the whole piece and concept richer and clearer. That's what we need in leaders, regardless of where they are.

So leaders, how are your artistic views?

Being Open to Proactive Serendipity Can Alter Your Future

February 28, 2017

Don't think too much when you answer this question:

As you review your career, what's an example of an unexpected encounter or piece of information that took you in a direction you had not anticipated?

Feel free to send me examples. I'd love to learn about them.

If you have one, or many, of those examples, you could be a victim of serendipity.

A few years ago, I sat next to a person at a fundraiser. We chatted, and then he realized that someone had mentioned me as a person who might help him in a small way with a project he was doing.

That unexpected encounter has led to a terrific relationship. I helped him with his project at several stages. He has given me new ways to think about risks I should take and encouraged me to take them. I often think about how lucky we were to sit next to each other. Serendipity in action.

But in fact, it is not enough just to have an unexpected encounter or to have a piece of information appear. For serendipity to happen in a positive way, we have to notice and decide whether to pursue that unexpected event.

I could have kept the conversation with my friend at a superficial level or said, "Oh no, I'm not the best person to help you with that project, but thanks for thinking of me." We would have enjoyed a nice meal and said goodbye.

But each of us made the effort to notice that this encounter might be valuable, and then we pursued it. At each stage, we could have finished and moved on, but we have continued to get together, push and learn from one another.

So what does it take for serendipity to happen?

I suspect there are a few key elements: We need to be open to and curious about experiences, information and encounters. If I assume that my world is enough, that I know the people I want to, or that I really don't need to do things differently, then I may be less willing to notice something unexpected.

But if I'm curious, open, alert and confident, then I'm more likely to recognize and then consider something unexpected. Then, if I evaluate that something, I could decide that "yes, this is something worth pursuing," or "no, not now or not ever." The key is that I was proactive about noticing and evaluating.

Now I wonder if this is something that organizations could build into their culture. More on that later.

In the meantime, try to notice unexpected events, people, and information and see if you can take advantage of "proactive serendipity."

What Are Your Organization's Values and Why Should You Care?

April 13, 2017

If you had to create a brand for yourself, based on the values you hold, what would it be?

Values are the foundation that drive your behaviors, your decisions, and make you appealing—or not—as a person others want to be around or be like. It's what you stand for.

Now think of a company you have had a remarkably negative experience with. What were your assumptions about that organization, after that experience? Go to the firm's website and see if it lists values of what the firm is or wants to be known for. Does the list match your experience? If not, that firm is in trouble.

Whether we like it or not, organizational values matter. Russ Stoddard, author of "Rise Up," says values are like pheromones, sending signals to customers and employees that say what your organization stands for.

He claims that some organizational leaders don't think deliberately enough when they create values and supporting statements. So he encourages leaders to take time and really consider what they want their organization's values to be.

He uses an example close to home, the city of Boise, which has the vision of being the country's "most livable city." The value statements clarify what that means using LIV as a trigger:

L: Lasting environments. Recognize, protect and improve the health and sustainability of all our activities, our connections to one another, and our natural resources.

I: Innovative enterprises. Work with individuals, nonprofits, and businesses to encourage creativity and collaboration that will promote economic prosperity and improve lives.

V: Vibrant communities. Engage citizens and organizations to spark new connections, inspire cooperation, and strengthen Boise's rich, community-minded spirit.

Keep in mind that organizations express those values in many ways — not just words on a poster or wall. Physical infrastructure and environment can help. If you think about Boise's first value of lasting environments, we see and experience the connections to each other (as a smaller, informal community) and to nature around us (the Greenbelt, the Foothills).

Why do all of this? As Stoddard says, employees and customers are increasingly looking for organizations to work with that give meaning, have a clear purpose, and make the experience exceptional.

So what are you waiting for? What are your values?

Why Are You in Business, Really?

March 24, 2017

Why are you in business? To make money, right?
For some leaders, it's not that simple anymore.

Russ Stoddard describes himself as "founder and president of Oliver Russell, a public benefit corporation that builds brands for purpose-driven companies whose products, services or business models benefit society." In that statement, he offers several key nuggets from his new book, "Rise Up: How to Build a Socially Conscious Business." It's available in an "early edition" at russstoddard.com. The book has several interesting points that I'll talk about over the coming weeks, but today, let's start with purpose.

Stoddard argues that it's not enough for organizations to have a mission or vision statement. More important is a purpose statement. That's because stakeholders—whether customers, employees and others—increasingly want to interact with firms that do something good, beyond just making money.

Rather than working "for a paycheck," which was more common a few decades ago, Stoddard says many people, especially entrepreneurs, work because of the passion and meaning they gain. As one local entrepreneur puts it, "I GET to do this work. I don't HAVE to do it." Also, Stoddard sees more leaders using the notion of purpose as a way to gain competitive advantage. Buying clothes from Patagonia assures great quality but for many people, it also supports an organization that respects the natural environment.

So what is "purpose?"

While mission statements tend to be "inward facing," giving employees a sense of business strategy and direction, purpose statements have a different focal point. According to Stoddard, purpose statements explain the reason or the "why" an organization does what it does, with a focus on looking outward. In particular, they explain how an organization will "make a difference in the lives of stakeholders."

He uses Patagonia's statement as an example:

"Build the best product, cause no unnecessary harm, use the business to inspire and implement solutions to the environmental crisis."

A well-written statement can inspire employees, and potential employees, as well.

Stoddard writes that on average, at least daily, someone contacts him about working at his firm. The person typically does not ask about specific jobs but instead says she or he is "inspired by the company."

As a professor, I can confirm his experience from the other side. Students frequently ask about some of the companies in town that inspire them—how could they get in, find out more, or perhaps work there in the future. Wouldn't you love to hear people say, "I'm so lucky. I GET to work at my firm."

So, once again, why are you in business, really?

You Can Find Joy at the Bottom of a Steep Learning Curve

November 1, 2016

To anyone who knows my household, it's clear who the chef is. Not me. But I found myself inspired by someone who does know his way around a kitchen.

Anthony Bourdain is a longtime chef who has also had several television shows and, most recently, is known for having lunch with Barack Obama in Hanoi. They ate Bun Cha, a dish with noodles, coriander, and pork— delicious, at a small place near the center of town. Last month I went by the restaurant, where they now offer the "Combo Obama" of Bun Cha and beer.

Bourdain is promoting a new cookbook, so he's on the promotion circuit. During one of the interviews he gave recently, he talked about his career and how he started as a dishwasher, which is probably par for most chefs who learn the value of the work ethic.

Then he made a statement that hit me hard:

"I still like being at the bottom of a steep learning curve."

Many people find joy in becoming very good at their jobs and careers. They like the comfort of staying within that field or position.

I get into an odd funk if I do the same thing too often or for too long. I experienced it a few days ago, just before I heard Bourdain's comment, when I realized I was very unexcited about something I was working on. Then I went into a meeting, feeling as though I was just dragging, as though I was carrying extra weight.

During the meeting, a new project idea came up, and we discussed how it might work. It involves a problem I never considered, in an area that is completely new to me, an area that needs some good thinking around it. We didn't quite get all details settled, so much of it still needs to be shaped. But when I left the meeting, I felt twenty pounds lighter.

What was the difference?

I was stepping into an area that I knew nothing about, where I would have a chance to learn something new. I found myself thrilled at the thought that I'm at the bottom of a steep learning curve.

I'm lucky in that I often can choose the learning curves I want to step into. Change in organizations is often thrust upon us, with no choice about learning fast.

But when the opportunity comes up, at least for me, I'll take the steep curve over the humming comfort of a job I know (too) well.

Is This All There Is? What Do You Do When You've Done What You Want?

November 23, 2016

Recently I talked with a group of leaders who have built and run high-performing and very creative organizations. Several of them had been hired years ago to turn around those same organizations. In one case, the leader managed to rebuild the organization much faster than expected.

So here they were, top of their careers, known for the work they are doing. Then one of them asked the group, "Is this it?"

And they all knew what he meant.

They're successful, have done what was expected and more, and now they are questioning what's next. Some worry about becoming bored. Others fear complacency.

So now what? Do they go to larger, more complex organizations, which would mean leaving the community that they love? Do they shift careers altogether and start at the bottom? If they stay in their current positions, can they find ways to make them more interesting, push the organizations in new directions?

After I heard this question, I started asking other leaders how they stay motivated and what keeps them from getting bored.

One said that, when he worked in a large organization that was growing, there were always new projects to be done, so he was never bored.

Another said his industry is always changing, so the company is forced to reinvent itself, and that means leaders and employees all need to change.

One had left his former organization to become a consultant in the field. In consulting, this leader said, "the problems are basically the same, but the context, culture, and people are different so I'm always learning."

Then I heard that one of my favorite journalists, Lucy Kellaway of the *Financial Times*, has decided to leave her columnist post after thirty-one years. She is beginning training to become a "maths teacher" in England. A very new shift, and she says she is excited—and terrified. But it's time to change and do something new.

In the end, what became clear is that these sharp leaders need to be in a situation where they are learning—whether that learning is imposed from the organization itself or whether they come up with a new task or challenge for themselves and the organization.

We should be thankful if we are in a position to ask the question, "Is this it?" But perhaps a final lesson is to ask it on a regular basis, rather than waiting till we need to make a shift.

Part 5

Behind the Scenes

Part 5: Behind the Scenes gives a glimpse into a couple of organizations that utilize creativity and culture in sometimes hidden ways. Boise State Football and the Boise Zoo have some important insight on how to keep business running smoothly.

What Happens Behind the Scenes at Zoo Boise

December 21, 2015

When a 350-pound sloth bear needs a root canal, how does Zoo Boise make it happen?

I've been looking behind the scenes around town – at the county jail, Boise State football games, and now, Zoo Boise, which is part of the Parks and Recreation Department of the city of Boise.

The 30 full- and part time employees and 300 volunteers (who donate 35,000 hours every year) help inspire and educate some 340,000 annual guests while also raising money for conservation of animals in the wild. Since 2007, in fact, Zoo Boise has generated $1.8 million for conservation. As a percentage of total revenues, that puts our zoo among the top donators in the world.

But when I heard that Paji, the female sloth bear, had a root canal in October, I was hooked.

Early one Tuesday morning, long before the zoo opened, the 5'5" tall bear was knocked out with a dart gun. It took 15-20 minutes for Paji to fall to the ground in her den. The zoo veterinarian, Dr. Holly Holman, tested the bear to make sure she was really out (by touching the area around her eyes; she didn't blink, so the bear was in dream land).

All of this happened before the bear's den had been cleaned, to keep her as calm as possible beforehand, so Paji fell into her own manure and whatever else had collected. Six staff members stepped through the muck on the ground, rolled the bear onto a cargo net, put her onto a red golf cart and motored off to the zoo hospital, officially called the Animal Health Complex. The vet weighed the bear on a 6-foot long scale to figure out how much anesthesia to use, cleaned her up, and then monitored vitals during the procedure.

The animal was stretched out on the surgery table in "bear rug fashion," stomach down, head out front. Since bear teeth are about 1.5" long, the team of two dentists and two techs used hefty files (not the wimpy ones used on humans). Afterward, staff members hauled Paji back to her den (by now cleaned up), where she spent the day recovering.

Another day in the life of a zoo animal and those who care for it.

On 11 acres, Zoo Boise is home to 107 species, including more than 300 animals, although the keepers count the "cockroach collection" as one animal. The exhibits range from the rainforest to one about animals who live on islands (all sorts of interesting evolutionary and scientific curiosities from those systems) to jellyfish and insects.

Nine zoo keepers oversee the animals and their living quarters, using checklists for daily, weekly and monthly tasks. The Rainforest area exhibit — which houses an Aldabra tortoise named Ms. Mac, along with sloths and spider monkeys — needs weekly raking of leaves, misting of indoor exhibits, replacement of wet soil, and removal of cobwebs, for instance.

And while many of the animals seem cuddly, the keepers know that these are wild animals, many quite dangerous. Behind the den of the Desert Exhibit's 9-foot-long Komodo Dragon, an intimidating sign — reflecting zookeeper humor — makes the point: BEWARE OF ATTACK LIZARD. Next to the door leading to the venomous snake and gila monster exhibits is an eye-level, ping-pong-ball-sized red button and a sign: PUSH IN CASE OF SNAKE BITE.

On the other hand, Julius the Giraffe was thrilled to get a cracker from his zookeeper, Leticia Herrera, and show off his 8" purple tongue in the process.

Some people despair that we even have zoos. But Director Steve Burns notes that zoos like this one raise over $160 million each year to save animals that might otherwise be killed or die off. Animals like the famed Galapagos Islands' tortoises would be long gone if it weren't for the humans who help breed and care for them.

And from a personal standpoint, visiting the zoo on a quiet December afternoon (it is open year round) was a perfect antidote to my hectic life, bringing me to a spot where I could think about nothing else for a few minutes but the feel of a purple tongue on my fingers.

Squeamish? Don't Read This.
Curious About Problem Solving?
Read This.

February 22, 2016

Reader alert: This column has a wee bit of an "eww" factor. If you are squeamish about food, or rather about what zoo animals eat, move on to sports or movies. But I'm fascinated by what one organization does in a super-efficient and effective manner that perhaps the rest of us could learn from.

Zoo Boise has 300 individual animal residents (the cockroach "collection" counts as one resident, however, and I'm not certain the zookeepers know how many butterflies there are). But for those other animals, take a guess at what the zoo spends on food every year? When I ask people that question, the guesses range from half a million to $2 million a year. Sit down.

The zoo spends about $125,000 a year feeding its animals, which works out to about $342 per day to feed those 300 plus residents. Granted, some eat every day (or twice a day like penguins), while others may eat every few weeks (the python), but still, that seems like good financial and operational management to me. I was curious how the zoo was able to do it.

First, some of the food is grown on site. Next time you visit, notice the bamboo plants. They are everywhere — the red pandas eat little else. The bamboo plants also provide some shade and natural fences between exhibits, and it just keeps on growing.

The "zoo kitchen" also grows some insects like mealworms and crickets. Sloth bears, those 350-pound black furry balls with the white "necklaces," love mealworms. When the zookeepers slide them into the exhibit through a pipe, the bears lumber over and then dig for them in the dirt.

Likewise, Patas monkeys go wild for crickets. They love to scamper around their dens catching them. It keeps their brains active as well.

In addition, the zoo buys much of its food from providers who make you smile or cringe, if you're not in the business. Krill for jellyfish. Smelt and kapelin for penguins. Insectivore diet, which looks like Grape-Nuts for anteaters. Bones for the big cats one day a week to keep the tartar off their teeth.

Then there are the pinkies.

Of course, every industry has its suppliers. I just never thought about what a zoo needed, especially when it comes to carnivores. Big cats eat horse meat, imported from Canada, since it resembles the game they would hunt in the wild. The python eats rabbits. The birds of prey (condor, eagle, hawk, owls) eat guinea pigs and other small rodents.

Sure enough, the supplier firms come through and even have (to the outsider) a sense of humor in their names. Companies like Rodent Pro or Gourmet Rodent supply frozen mice, rats, rabbits and guinea pigs. And the last time I checked Rodent Pro's website, there was a sale on extra-small pinky mice, 17 cents each. They are called "pinkies" because they are pink, but also because they are about the size and look of the last knuckle of a man's pinky finger. The frozen rodents, along with some fruit and vegetables, rest in shelves in the zoo kitchen's industrial-size freezer.

So what on earth could business organizations learn from the zoo's food operations?

The biggest idea I take away is the ability the zoo has to solve several problems with one solution. Using bamboo as food, as a barrier to carve off areas within the physical space, and as a welcome shade provider in the summer solves three problems, and is also cost-effective. Likewise, crickets as a food source, but also as a way to stimulate the monkeys' brains, solves multiple problems.

So how do other organizations get a three-for-one type of benefit? Start looking in yours.

How We Idahoans Can Help Save Wild African Animals

March 30, 2017

Steve Burns, director of Zoo Boise, thinks about animals "all the time…it causes me great pain to see what's happening with so many of the animals that I think about."

Burns' particular worry is that animals in the wild are disappearing. A World Wildlife Fund study says the total number of animals in the wild, like elephants and giraffes, tigers and rhinos, plummeted by 58 percent between 1970 and 2015.

Since most of us will never see those animals in the wild, zoos offer a chance to see and learn about them firsthand. But too many face extinction because of humans. The number of elephants, for instance, fell from 1.3 million in 1980 to 450,000 in 2015. Even worse, they are disappearing at a rate of 96 per day, mostly because of poaching. Giraffe number have dropped 30 percent in the same period, to fewer than 100,000.

Burns' and Zoo Boise's concern for the vulnerable have helped our zoo become a leader in wildlife conservation. The zoo started the notion of a "conservation fee" nine years ago that now generates about $300,000 per year, and more than $2.2 million over the last nine years, to support conservation of animals in the wild.

The bulk of that money goes to saving a national park in Mozambique called Gorongosa. As recently as 15 years ago, the park had fewer than 1,000 hoofed animals, thanks to wars and poverty. Humans made (or felt they had to make) choices that obliterated the animal population. Twenty years of war meant soldiers traipsing through the Gorongosa nature preserve; they had to eat, and the hoofed animals were available.

Elephants, hippos, antelope, buffalo and waterbuck all disappeared. After the war finished, a few animals returned, but humans continued to decimate them. Villagers surrounding the preserve faced starvation, so they scoured the land for food. Once again, human choices and needs overwhelmed the animals' survival.

Thanks to a major benefactor, Idaho's Greg Carr, and efforts of many partnerships, the park has come back.

Villages surrounding the preserve now are part of an increasingly thriving economic network and ecosystem. Skills training, education and jobs that support tourism mean villagers don't need to eat the animals. The control of poaching fosters animal survival. Today, Gorongosa is again becoming one of the world's greatest national parks, with more than 80,000 hoofed animals.

It is a remarkable story of turning science, economics and cultural sensitivity into actions to stop what could have been widespread extermination and extinction of several species.

Partly to celebrate, and partly to help us learn more about the park, Zoo Boise is raising funds to build a Gorongosa exhibit. It will bring a little bit of the Mozambican park to us, including some of my favorite Gorongosa animals: African wild dogs, crowned cranes and warthogs.

The campaign is in its final days to raise money to receive a matching $1.5 million. (I've made a donation). Let's hope they make it.

How to Put on a Boise State Football Game? Start with Shirts

September 4, 2015

What happens behind the scenes at a football game? More than you may think

If you are going to the Boise State-Washington football game tonight, or even watching on TV, chances are you'll have a touch of color to show which side you favor. I'll be wearing my blue sparkle ballet shoes along with a hint of orange.

But many people go straight for the hard core: t-shirts that scream Boise State or "the other team." Some of you may even wear the game day "conversational t" – the one that says

WELCOME TO THE BLUE.
NO DAWGS ALLOWED.

Good start to the season.

Not so fast. In fact, while we fans may think it's the start, the real work has gone on for a lot longer.

To even GET to the "start of the season," hundreds of people have worked for months (or longer) to prepare for this single game and all those that come after. Imagine what goes into it—from security and parking, to tickets and promotion, lighting and music, choreography and food, media and medical support….and that's before you get to the football end of things—"costumes and props," videos and recruits, events and donors. And I'm not even counting the players and coaches!

This fall, I'll be doing a series of blogs about the behind the scenes operations of putting on a football game, the parts fans don't see and rarely think about, largely because it's done so well. I'm curious about the people and processes that make it work.

So we'll start what seems simple—the t-shirt you wear for the game.

The decision about t-shirts and color schemes started months before tonight. Representatives from the trademark licensing office, athletics marketing, football program and university bookstore meet in February or March, make decisions on the fan color schemes so they can order shirts for fall. If the shirts are Nike sponsored, though, the timeline is even longer—18 months before the season's start!

So that shirt you don today was born six months or more than a year ago!

But some shirts have a different, unsavory life.

Rachael Bickerton is Boise State's Director of Trademark Licensing and Enforcement. Her title is twofold, for a reason. As the university's "#1 worrier" about the university's trademark and brand, she works with more than 375 official licensees, from Nike to local crafters.

But sometimes, counterfeits sneak in, so on game day, Bickerton becomes the university's"#1 enforcer" of the trademark.

Her main priority is to stop unlicensed merchandise being sold. She keeps an eye out for bootleggers and for people engaging in any unauthorized commercial activity on campus before or during the game. Think: people selling cookies or shirts, offering face painting or handing out coupons for a free massage. When it's not university sanctioned, it's not going to stay on campus.

Bickerton has to be so firm for several reasons. Sales of officially licensed merchandise help support student scholarships and athletic programs. Given Boise State's modest budget, the additional money is crucial. Counterfeit merchandise drains support from the university and lines the pockets of infringers.

Second, she wants the atmosphere at the games and around the tailgate parties to be unmarred by hawkers. Official sponsors can operate in a specific area, in front of the Allen Noble Hall, but not elsewhere.

And last, of course, she wants the Boise brand to stay strong.

So this evening, watch for people pulling t-shirts out of backpacks or selling ones draped over their arms. Look out for hats that have the Bronco facing the wrong way with the wrong eye. And then step away!

Instead, put on that No Dawgs Allowed shirt (or another color that will go unnamed), have fun and cheer like mad.

How Ten Seconds Can Give You a Better Football Experience

September 17, 2015

The university wants us to be safe so we can have fun.

I never worry about safety at a football game maybe because I've never HAD to. I hope I never do. And 10 seconds may make the difference.

A sellout football game at Boise State brings together about 50,000 people into a 175 acre space for about six hours. That's 36,000 ticket holders and another 15-20,000 tailgaters who never even see the inside of the stadium.

It's a place where we all want to have a good time. But unfortunately, we also live in a world where stadiums and sports venues are attractive targets for criminal and terrorist activity.

This fall, my student assistant Madison Motzner and I are learning about what goes on behind the scenes at a football game. I got curious because it all seems to work so well that I hardly notice it as a fan. And one reason is the people who work hard to keep us safe so we can have a great experience.

We talked with several of the people who make this work—from university managers like Dave Ellis and John Kaplan to Mark Vucinich, owner of the security firm MAV, and some of his employees. We wanted to learn about what they do to help prevent harm of all sorts, from injuries to other threats.

Large professional sports venues, like NFL or baseball stadiums, have long had systematic security—from stadium sweeps and metal detectors to chemical experts and police forces. But even smaller venues, like Boise State, need to be prepared.

So what happens here?

For football games, the university works with the company MAV, which brings in over 300 security people, in addition to 40-60 Boise Police Department officers, and about 10 university experts. On top of that, many other agencies help out—federal to local. And we have metal detectors—one of the first universities to take that step. Evidently, it's worked well for us, so far.

In fact, in 2015, Albertsons Stadium at Boise State University won a merit award from the National Center for Spectator Sports Safety and Security (NCS4) for its systematic and successful security (other 2015 winners included Auburn and University of California, Berkeley, not bad company).

But sometimes, we fans make the job of keeping us safe hard for those who want to protect us. Apparently, 20 minutes before the game, some 60% of ticket holders, or 20,000 people on a big day, are NOT in the stadium, and think they can breeze through security to reach their seats before kickoff. No wonder some fans get testy, or worse.

The search of your bag and walk through a metal detector doesn't take long, usually about 8-10 seconds, assuming you don't need to be wanded. And this happens for everyone entering the stadium, which is about 1200-1300 people per gate per game. The security folks work fast but we need to help them out—maybe head to our seats 10 minutes earlier, realize we're in "airport mode" even in the stadium, and be grateful that we can relax and enjoy the game because of these people.

Perhaps "nothing bad happens in Boise" because of what these folks do and so much else we may never see. It could be that ten seconds that makes a difference.

Behind the Scenes at a Boise State Football Game 101

September 30, 2015

How does Boise State organize a football game day? With lots of groups together off the field, most of which you'll never notice if they do it right.

Imagine planning a wedding for 1000 guests—invitations, clothing, food, party favors, music, dancing, security, preparing (and cleaning up) the facility, parking, transporting elderly guests, managing social media, and following "rules" when it comes to seating assignments.

Now imagine doing all this—and more--for over 35,000 people six times in a four-month period and you'll get about 10% of the way to understanding what goes on behind the scenes at a Boise State home football game.

Each time my student assistant Madison Motzner and I talk to one of the people who make the game day experience so great, we're overwhelmed…again.

Putting on a football game involves at least 14 different operational areas, not including the program itself (e.g., recruiters, trainers, "costume and props"). We're talking media to tickets, security to parking, marketing to concessions, the band/cheer/dance squad to compliance. And they all have to coordinate.

So what are a few of those behind the scenes elements? Let me give you a tiny peek.

Bob Carney, Associate Athletic Director/Operations, oversees about 130 on-site NCAA competitions annually across the 20 sports that 397 Boise State student athletes engage in. Each sport has its own manual and checklist to be sure things are done according to NCAA, Mountain West Conference and Boise State rules. The football manual, for example, is 6" thick--300 double-sided pages. Carney's involved in everything from stadium "lock down" a week before a game to overseeing clean up afterward, which requires six 40-yard dumpsters for recycling and trash.

Assistant Athletic Director Matt Thomas manages marketing and promotions on the screens and the field (think "Ford punt truck"). He has 250-300 "script lines" of what promotion goes where, at what time, and for how long (10-60 seconds). He also coordinates media breaks, time outs, and even monitoring the time it takes the band onto the field (55 seconds). In addition, he oversees social media around sports, making sure Boise State's 120,000 Facebook followers and 30,000 Twitter followers get the information they want.

For 20 years, Bob Royce has worked with the 65 ticket takers and ushers on game day, helping people find seats, settle disagreements (1 or 2 per game) and have a great time. He walks 19,000 steps during a game, and assures me you can enter almost any gate and get to the other side of the stadium from the inside.

Associate Athletic Director for Development Dusty Clements helps the Bronco Athletic Association raise scholarship money for student athletes, but also gets involved in game day activities. His crew does things like oversee the 1500 reserved tailgate spots, transport guests who are unable to walk easily, and wipe down the orange seats in the stadium that season pass holders buy for the fall. They also help BAA members solve problems ("I am driving in from McCall and just noticed I forgot my tickets").

The longtime ticket office guru, Anita Guerricabeitia, runs the selling of about 240,000 football tickets per season (36,000 times six plus any extra games) and tickets for the other sports, including basketball, gymnastics and wrestling, track and field and so many more. Given that some 2000 football season ticket buyers change their seats each year, she also manages the "relocation event" that happens in the spring where people decide on new seats, and often, buy more.

NCAA Compliance plays a big role throughout the academic year but also for games. Associate Athletic Director of Compliance, Matt Brewer quotes his five year-old daughter in how she explains his job: "my dad makes sure the Broncos follow the rules." Indeed. Given that the NCAA generates about 20 new rules a year and each rule may have 10-15 "interpretations," he's got to be on top of what athletes, coaches, donors—and even academic staff—can do relating to student athletes and potential recruits. He monitors everything from who can be on the sidelines before the game (boosters on the visitor side, recruits on the home side) and insures that all leave the field before kickoff to how many coaches and others can "talk into headsets" (i.e., coach) versus just listen in.

As Bob Carney says, "we do our jobs well when people come to a game, leave and never knew what happened behind the scenes." It's all about having a great experience. What a treat.

How Boise State Football Satisfies "Hunger"

October 23, 2015

How do Boise State communications and culinary staff handle our hunger for information and food?

Two types of hunger prevail when it comes to football games: hunger for information and hunger for food. Boise State's experts on both surprised me once again on just what goes on "behind the scenes."

Joe Nickell, Assistant Athletic Director for Communications, and Max Corbet, his predecessor and current Assistant Athletic Director for Administration, estimate that about 30 media outlets want information about Boise State during game weeks. They range from local, regional and national TV and radio stations to websites and newspapers--from ESPN to the Idaho Statesman. So Nickell and his staff start by preparing and updating the 40 page thick Game Notes, a compilation of statistics about previous games, seasons, and information about the upcoming game. It includes everything from new stats and trends to clippings and comparisons of Boise State with other teams over the season and years to how to pronounce players' names. One note I love is that Boise State has received, for the last five years, an NCAA award for academic success, along with such powerhouses as Clemson, Duke and Northwestern. Not bad company. The game notes make any media person who takes time to study them much smarter about the games, which means their commentary and questions can be more on target as well.

Then there are the interviews. Nickell estimates that coaches and athletes spend 7-8 hours in front of a microphone in a week, excluding the time it takes to set up and prepare for the interviews. Head Coach Bryan Harsin alone likely spends 5-6 hours, what with his press conferences, weekly TV show, meeting with the national media and those from the opposing team's region, and the during and immediate post-game interviews. The staff also manages social media interactions, no small feat with 160,000 Twitter impressions per day about the program.

There's also the literal hunger on game day itself. Fans devour about 3500 Double R Ranch hot dogs, 2500 soft pretzels, 5500 bottles of water, and 1200 gallons of popcorn on game day, along with 1000 catered meals (in the Hall of Fame, the Stueckle Sky Center, at the SUB, and for the media). For the upcoming game against Wyoming, look for 1800 pounds of beef in the chili you may eat.

Philippe Didier, Executive Chef for Aramark, who contracts with Boise State, recently received the Pro Chef II certification from the Culinary Institute of America, the gold standard of the cooking world. He plans menus in the spring for fall games. Then, during game week, he orders food on Wednesday, it arrives on Thursday and preparation begins Friday (e.g., thawing, marinades). Twelve hours before a Saturday game kickoff, he and six other chefs are hard at work with "prep, fire, box, and serve" after transferring food from the Student Union to the kitchen underneath the stands in the Sky Center. Along with Aramark's General Manager for Boise State, Carol Scott, they oversee some 155 people who provide and serve the food and clean up, which can take up to six hours following the game.

And they do all of this with aplomb. The temperature in last year's San Diego game, 15 November 2014, dipped to 9 degrees, so cold that the concession pipes froze during the game: that meant no sodas, no coffee, no cocoa. So, the staff began racing to the SUB kitchen to make the drinks and warm food they knew people would need. Crisis averted.

That's "behind the scenes" in action. Fans had a great experience and most never knew what might have gone wrong.

A Look at Costumes and Props (aka Uniforms and Equipment) at a Boise State Football Game

November 9, 2015

When I met Dale Holste, certified athletic equipment manager for Boise State, to learn about football "costumes and props," he chuckled. His sister works in theater.

Holtste, at Boise State since 1996, oversees uniforms and equipment for 110 players and 25 coaches. Sliding storage cabinets — 12 feet tall, 4 feet deep — hold over 600 sets of uniforms, 500 helmets, 2,000 gloves and more.

Each player has five helmets, one for practice and four for games — blue, black, orange, white. They are fitted to a player's head by pumping air into three sets of air pads at the back, top and jaw. When the team plays in higher or lower altitudes, the air sacs are filled or emptied accordingly. Face masks are titanium or lightweight steel. Players have five game-day jerseys and pants (grey, white, blue, black and orange). You need to do math to figure out many variations they have.

Front-line players who shove and take hard hits wear gloves like Wolverine hands without the long knives: hard plastic padding on the knuckles and long finger bones, and strips down the backhand. Game shoes (four sets per person — orange and white or blue and black, for grass or turf) get their own room: 250 pairs, stacked 12 feet high.

A helmet and uniform can weigh up 9 pounds.

Holste also stores the 10 Boise footballs used each week, with officials' marks that they are approved.

This is the part we see. Then there's the prep and clean up.

If you've ever complained about laundry, don't in front of Holste. Weight-room workout clothes, practice uniforms and two towels per player are all sorted, washed and rebundled daily for 135 people. His staff runs 14 loads of laundry – 60 pounds each – nearly every day, and more on game day. At two hours per load, the laundry keeps the five washers and 10 dryers busy for hours. And just like the rest of us, he worries about grass stains, blood, and making his players and coaches look good.

So next game, take a moment to marvel at another behind-the-scenes element that makes football theater such a kick.

How Athletic Trainers Keep the Football Game Going at Boise State

November 19, 2015

After the Boise State-New Mexico football game, I got a note from Marc Paul, assistant athletic director and head athletic trainer for Boise State. At 1:35 a.m., roughly 90 minutes after the game ended, he and his sports-medicine staff were finally leaving for the night.

They would return nine hours later to help get players ready for another game in six days. There are "more things to treat the day after a loss than a win," he said, so Sunday would be busy.

I suspect Paul meant that more injuries happen in losses, but after talking with and watching him and his staff over about six hours, it became clear that they care about more than just physical repairs. Once again, I was privileged to watch a behind-the-scenes group that is critical to the football experience. Two full-time athletic trainers, Jim Spooner and Paul Smith, plus nine students keep the football student athletes in good working order. Ten other athletic trainers and 25 students work with the other 300-plus athletes.

Their facility includes an antigravity machine (like walking on the moon), which allows a 200-pound athlete to "run" in a 130-pound body so his ankle can heal. An underwater treadmill pool's five cameras track stride, sideways movement and gait. Tables for taping, stretching, repairing … all in natural light and calmness that explodes expectations built on seeing those cramped sweaty training rooms in boxing movies.

Here's some of what I learned:

On game day, from 5:55 p.m. to 8:21 p.m. (the scheduled kick off), 20 lines on a laminated schedule describe who is where, doing what, when.

From about 6:15 to 7:10, three or four athletic trainers tape about 100 ankles, taking two to three minutes for each ankle, applying adhesive spray, then padding, then blue or black tape that "sticks to itself." For some players, on go the socks, then more tape around the shoe through the cleats. The trainers start sweating about 15 minutes into this gig, peeling off their own outer shirts. Some players get knee braces (not a favorite), some have taping on their wrists, thighs, torsos. Athletic trainers stretch players into pretzel positions. The room is busy but calm.

Starting 83 minutes before kick off (6:58), some position group is on the field every 3 or 5 or 10 minutes. In between, players return for more taping, for a new mouth guard, or adjusting of a brace.

The staff heads to the field after the players run through fog shot out of what looks like an 18-inch-diamter, 6-foot long stainless-steel canister. A Powerade station and chicken-broth containers are ready. Water bottles await on the benches for players to grab and gulp. The student assistants roam around with more water, encouraging player hydration to avoid cramps.

All around me, microstories unfold. Redshirt freshmen, wearing jerseys and jeans, flap white towels and cheer with the crowd. Players who miss a catch — or make one — get a shoulder nudge or helmet slap. Four throw a ball back and forth about 2 feet from my head. A quarterback answers one of two phones that look like old office-table models.

I watch the athletic trainers, since it's tough to see the real game (not the screen game). While standing on the sidelines may be cool, I feel like I'm in a forest of black-

and-blue-uniformed trees, a foot or two taller than I am. They didn't look this big in the training room.

The trainers scout for who's slow to stand up, limping, anything unusual. They first watch the front-line players, because they are likely to push and shove the longest. Then they check the second and third layer. All in seconds.

One player is hit, and Smith grabs the edge of his shoulder pad to pull him aside. Smith has a bushy beard better suited to working with smoke jumpers (which he has done). He stands 6 inches from the player's face, asks him questions to keep the young man's focus on him, and finally nudges him inside for a check. A second trainer tells the coach in charge so personnel changes can be made, fast.

Another player hurts his ankle. Spooner and team doctor Kirk Lewis create a bubble of calm around the player, who keeps his mouth from grimacing but looks disappointed. Spooner walks him to the training facility, and by half time, the tape is off and the player's foot is encased in what appears to be a flannel ice pad. Two friends sit on the table next to the player. A trainer checks on him. Again, calmness pervades.

When serious injuries happen, coaches (and others) get stressed, yet the athletic trainers keep things calm with an intense focus and presence that makes me think they can forget about yoga. They are plenty "in the moment" during those games.

Spooner, like all of the people in this group, is quick to praise people he works with — fellow athletic trainers, the team doctor, players. Members of the sports-medicine staff look after each other, as well as the players. This is not a "me" culture. It's one where they try to build relationships, have an impact and learn.

At the end of the night, the trainers compare notes on who's been hurt and how badly, and who needs MRIs or X-rays. They drive home already thinking about "injury triage" on Sunday and the countdown to the next game.

Acknowledgments

Even small books are a product of many people and much support. This book is a collection of blogs and columns, slightly edited, that have appeared in the *Idaho Statesman* over the last several years. But it started much earlier.

The notion of writing—or speaking—to audiences other than students or academics started for me when Jim East, program manager at Boise State Public Radio (KBSX 91.5), now senior vice president for development, Colorado Public Radio, asked Boise State's Professor Gundars Kaupins and me to write and deliver a daily business-focused program, *Idaho Business Matters*. Learning how to make a point in two hundred words and say it without mistakes took me a long time, but thanks to Boise State Public Radio's engineer extraordinaire Erik Jones, he made it sound great every single day.

The radio program ran from 2006 to 2012 and became a springboard for a next learning experience and challenge, writing a column for print and then digitally for the *Idaho Statesman*. Business editor Dave Staats was open to the notion of my doing it on a weekly basis, so we started an adventure in 2013 that has continued since. Dave has allowed me to dabble in areas that range from whitewater rafting and science lessons for business leaders, to ways to learn and keep curiosity fresh. His encouragement to try new ideas and his patience when I find "one more typo" at the last minute that needs to be corrected makes him the dream editor.

Boise State University has been my intellectual home for almost three decades. The best home is one that encourages curiosity and travel, expansion of thinking and lack of severe boundaries. But it is also the place to return to for nourishment. I have had that and more from the leaders and colleagues I've worked with and known. Thank you to all of them.

Many others deserve thanks as well. Students and business leaders have long let me pick their brains for ideas and questions. Stephanie Chism managed the Centre for Creativity and Innovation, which provided many opportunities to test ideas and bring them to a bigger world. Madison Motzner, Boise State honors student, has reached from her science world to our business world and become a one-person production company, learning how to put together small books that we hope will have big impact. Thanks, Madison, for making this one happen.

References

Learning from Unexpected Sources

Page 18: Bar-Eli, M., Azar, O. H., Ritov, I., Keidar-Levin, Y., and G. Schein. 2007. "Action Bias among Elite Soccer Goalkeepers: The Case of Penalty Kicks." *Journal of Economic Psychology* 28 (5): 606–21.

Page 66: Bunge, J. 2016. "Farmers Reap New Tools From Their Own High-Tech Tinkering." *The Wall Street Journal.*

Page 42: Fields, D. R. 2014. "Myelin-More than Insulation." *Science* 344 (6181): 264-266.

Page 66: Gura, T. 2014. "The art of entrepreneurship." *Science* 346 (6213): 1146.

Page 60: Page Hamers, R. 2015. "ING chief executive: Digital but down-to-earth." *Financial Times.*

Page 44: Leslie, I. 2014. *Curious.* New York, NY: Basic Books.

Page 18: Van Tilburg, W. A. P., and E. R.. 2011. "On Boredom and Social Identity: A Pragmatic Meaning-Regulation Approach." *Personality and Social Psychology Bulletin* 37 (12): 1679–91.

Page 47: Well +Good (wellandgood.com) reports on the top 16 health, fitness, and nutrition trends to be talked about in 2016.

About the Author

Nancy K. Napier, distinguished professor and former director of the Centre for Creativity and Innovation at Boise State University and adjunct professor at Aalborg University (Denmark). She scours the world for ideas—from Vietnam to Botswana. Mostly, she loves the ones from unexpected places, like zoos and football coaches.